GW00707514

RHODESIANA REPRINT LIBRARY—
SILVER SERIES

Volume 3

RHODESIANA REPRINT LIBRARY—
SILVER SERIES

Rhodesia of To-day

A Description of the Present Condition and the
Prospects of Mashonaland & Matabeleland

by

E. F. KNIGHT

Rhodesiana Reprint Library – Silver Series
Volume Three

Facsimile reproduction of the 1895 edition
with new Foreword and illustrations

BOOKS OF RHODESIA
BULAWAYO 1975

BOOKS OF RHODESIA PUBLISHING CO. (PVT.) LTD.

P.O. Box 1994, Bulawayo.

Publishers of Rhodesiana Reprints
and New Rhodesian Literary Works

ISBN 0 86920 123 9

PRINTED IN RHODESIA BY MARDON PRINTERS (PVT.) LTD., BULAWAYO

RE-PUBLICATION of this book has been made possible by the assistance of two Rhodesians of a Pioneer family whose wish it is that it be

dedicated to

THE RHODESIA PIONEERS' AND EARLY SETTLERS' SOCIETY

to honour the men and women who pioneered Rhodesia, and to promote a wider interest in the country's history.

The publishers gratefully acknowledge this help and have pleasure in making this out-of-print Rhodesiana work available to the public of Rhodesia through this Books of Rhodesia series.

FOREWORD TO REPRINT EDITION

EDWARD FREDERICK KNIGHT was born in 1852. After taking a B.A. degree at Caius College, Cambridge, he embarked on a distinguished career as an overseas correspondent of the *Morning Post*. He covered several important campaigns: Kitchener's Soudan Expedition of 1898; the South African War, in which he lost his right arm; and the Russo-Japanese conflict of 1904. His last post was in Turkey, where he reported on the 1908 Balkan crisis. The author of over twenty books, usually based on his despatches, he died after a lengthy retirement in 1925.

It is likely that *The Times* had sent out Knight initially to cover the Matabele War, thinking that the rains would delay operations against the powerful Ndebele until the dry season of 1894. However, the invasion had been effected with surprising ease, and Bulawayo fell several weeks before his arrival in January 1894. Knight accordingly spent the next seven months touring the country, investigating its development and prospects. This rather slender work is a compilation of the articles written during his travels and which had earlier appeared in *The Times*, although re-cast for publication in book form. The author has in general terms produced a work which in retrospect paints an over-sanguine picture of Rhodesia between the War and the 1896 Risings.

Like many observers, Knight was misled by the apparent willingness of the Ndebele to accept Company rule into disagreeing with the older hands about the possibility of further trouble. He shared the contemporary view of most that the Ndebele had gained a wholesome awe of the white man and welcomed an end to what the early settlers termed Lobengula's tyranny. But, as Sir Richard Martin later pointed out in his report on the Rising, the Ndebele had 'never been thoroughly subdued'; a few 'regiments' had been destroyed in the War, but others, while acquiescing to the invaders, had simply hidden away their weapons for a future opportunity. Likewise, Knight scouts the possibility of a Shona rising, commenting with an optimism that now seems facile that the War had 'taught the Mashonas that the white men are people to be respected' (p. 6).

As he was only a visitor to Rhodesia, the author might be excused these manifest errors of prediction; except for a small handful of the more percipient, the early settlers laboured under similar illusions. However, his vision was further obscured by an uncritical admiration of the Chartered Company, the growth of which had been noticeable in his later contributions to *The Times* and reached full bloom in this book. He consistently supports the Administration against its critics both at home and abroad, and accepts at face value its statements on African policy and reports on Rhodesia's potential as a gold producer. His book eventually becomes little more than a prospectus for potential miners and settlers, and Knight himself a promoter for the Chartered Company. Its propaganda value is enhanced further by the international reputation of Knight's employer, *The Times*, and its author's avoidance of the high-flown epithets that characterise other pro-Company works of the period.

Knight's comments on the Company's labour recruitment policy, land alienations in Matabeleland, farming and gold-mining prospects either minimised or ignored the actual situation in Rhodesia. That he was aware of the forced labour allegations being made by its critics is borne out by the text (p. 16), but apart from quoting official pronouncements, he does not take the matter any further. A more determined, less credulous journalist would have unearthed evidence to the contrary; since eight out of fifteen Native Commissioners questioned by Martin in 1897 admitted 'in unhesitating language' that they had ordered out labour, the practice could hardly have been a closely-guarded secret.

In his remarks on the wholesale allocation of farms in Matabeleland after the War, the author obscures the situation with a bland comment that there was plenty of land on the high veld for black and white. He goes on to say that the Ndebele 'have been told that they can return to those portions of the High Veldt which they occupied before the War . . . save where circumstances render a different course advisable'. In the event, the qualification overcame the initial promise: by 1898, the high veld Ndebele had become tenants of the landowners, many of them under-capitalised land companies, or were left with a few small reserves. Doubtless the author's prejudices against large reserves were responsible for his complacency, together with his strange notion that the movement of Africans to 'new locations' would be no hardship, as it was consonant with the exigencies of traditional shifting cultivation. Certainly, 'new locations' were found for the Ndebele in the arid and remote Shangani and Gwaai reserves, delimited in 1894, but by no stretch of the imagination could they be described as 'lands as favourable for grazing and agricultural purposes as those they (were) asked to surrender' (pp. 15-16).

A large part of this book is devoted to gold-mining. Knight arrived at a critical stage in Rhodesia's economic development. Hopes had been severely shaken by the first disappointing returns from the Mashonaland goldfields, where in fact most of the readily accessible deposits had been mined by the Shona several centuries earlier. A large number of fortune-seekers had gone to Matabeleland after the conquest in search of Eldorado. The author glosses over the discouraging Mashonaland situation, finding excuses that do not always ring true. It is difficult to see how the 'Matabele problem' could have affected the labour supply at Rezende and Penhalonga (p. 92), for example, since the Ndebele had not come within 80 miles of the area, even before the Occupation. Later in this chapter, Knight states that J. Hayes Hammond, the Company's mining adviser then investigating the goldfields, was favourably impressed with their prospects. Perhaps Hammond changed his mind later, as his report, published in November 1894 and some time before the appearance of the present work, disclosed that Rhodesia was, contrary to expectation, no 'Second Rand'. In a recent article[1], Ian Phimister of the University of Rhodesia has described how Rhodes 'distorted the tenor' of Hammond's report, and gave a credulous annual meeting of Chartered Company shareholders in early 1895 the impression that there were 'hundreds of miles of mineralised veins' in Rhodesia. Knight was in great measure a party to this deception, either by design or default, and one passage in the present work is strongly suggestive:

'The experts I met declared that in no other country they know of is there so much visible gold as in Matabeleland . . . it would be an unprecedented phenomenon were all these reefs to pinch out. It would be as if Nature had planned a cruel practical joke on a gigantic scale, with which to befool the world's gold-seekers' (pp. 80-1).

An inspired guess, or something more? Nature had indeed planned, and played, such 'a cruel practical joke', and although it transpired that Rhodesia had more abundant resources than its severest critics maintained—in 1908, gold production was worth £2½ m.—it certainly came nowhere near matching the Witwatersrand.

This contribution by a professional newspaperman to

[1]I. R. Phimister, 'Rhodes, Rhodesia and the Rand', *Journal of Southern African Studies*, 1, 1, October 1974, (pp. 74-90).

early Rhodesiana raises an interesting subsidiary topic, the Company's relations with Fleet Street and its use of the press to foster the Rhodesian enterprise. In his appreciation of its ability to create a favourable public image, Rhodes anticipated more recent times. By the end of 1894, he had won over nearly all the non-Radical bastions of the British press. His endeavours were aided by an influential group of journalists and publicists, most prominent of whom were Vere Stent, Lionel Decle and Flora Shaw of *The Times* (later privy to Rhodes's plans for the Uitlander rising and Jameson Raid). Some were motivated by his imperial vision and overlooked Rhodes the financier, while others were inspired by baser motives. But all, including Knight, were exploited to sustain the Company's image in the public eye at a crucial stage of its plans. They disseminated Jameson's rosy and often misleading reports on mining prospects in Rhodesia, becoming accessories (consciously or unconsciously) to the deception of the British investing public.

Was Edward Frederick Knight a willing tool or an unwilling dupe of the Chartered Company? Some of the evidence on the first charge is suggestive, but not altogether conclusive. His book was probably in the press when the Hammond report appeared and, in any case, Knight may have allowed himself to be swayed against its findings by Rhodes's remarks mentioned earlier. Nevertheless, one may fairly expect the insertion of at least some reference to the report at the end of the Preface, and the author stands accused of professional negligence at the very least. On the second charge, abundant evidence has been adduced to show that Knight was a dupe, and a willing dupe, of the Chartered administration. In this respect, he was in good company.

The present work is thus of interest to the present-day reader as a sample, somewhat more subtly presented than most, of the sanguine literature on Rhodesia's prospects that appeared in the early 1890s and ironically contributed to the disillusionment that followed the Jameson Raid, the 1896 Risings and the final disclosure that Rhodesia was, after all, not the anticipated Second Rand.

M. C. STEELE
Lecturer,
History Department,
University of Rhodesia.

Salisbury,
April 1975.

©

ILLUSTRATIONS

MATABELELAND & MASHONALAND

RHODESIA OF TO-DAY

A DESCRIPTION OF THE PRESENT CONDITION
AND THE PROSPECTS OF

MATABELELAND & MASHONALAND

BY

E. F. KNIGHT

AUTHOR OF 'WHERE THREE EMPIRES MEET' 'THE CRUISE OF THE FALCON' ETC.
RECENTLY CORRESPONDENT FOR 'THE TIMES' IN THE BRITISH
SOUTH AFRICA COMPANY'S TERRITORY

LONDON
LONGMANS, GREEN, AND CO.
AND NEW YORK : 15 EAST 16th STREET
1895

PREFACE

For the first seven months of this year, that is, for nearly the whole of the rainy season and for a considerable portion of the dry, I was travelling in Matabelelan d and Mashonaland. I entered the country by way of Tati and Bùlu-wayo, and, after having wandered some twelve hundred miles throughout its length and breadth, went out by Manica and Beira. I was thus enabled to gain a fair knowledge of this the first occupied and first to be developed portion of the vast territories which are within the sphere of the British South Africa Company's operations. It is my intention to summarise my experiences in this little work, and to present a general survey of the country as I found it. On my return to the Cape Colony and to England I met

numbers of people who were anxious to learn
from me all they could concerning the region I
had left ; among these were miners from California and Australia, traders, farmers, artisans, men
of all degrees and conditions, who were being
attracted to South Africa by the Matabeleland
boom. They said with justice that, hearing so
many contradictory reports, it was a most difficult matter for them to arrive at the truth.
Was Mashonaland, they asked in their perplexity,
the healthiest country in the world, or was it as
pestilential as the West Coast ; were the Matabele goldfields to surpass all others, or was there
but a delusive sprinkling of surface gold ; was
the Beira route into the country the most advantageous one, or had the railway proved a complete
fiasco ; and did the majority of travellers perish
when wading through the malarious swamps of
the tsetse fly belt which lie between the High Veldt
and the present terminus of the Beira railway ?
I found that even among generally well-informed

people in South Africa there existed a remarkable misapprehension of the facts, and a very
natural distrust of all the conflicting rumours
that came down-country.

In another work I purpose to give the history of the Chartered Company's vast enterprise;
but in this little book I will merely endeavour,
while bearing in mind the numerous questions
that were put to me by intending emigrants and
others interested in Matabeleland and Mashonaland, to briefly set forth the conditions that will
be met with in both territories, to give such
results of my information as may be of service to
some of those sanguine adventurers who are at
present flocking into what once was the kingdom
of Lobengula.

My thanks are due to the Editor of 'The
Times' for the permission he has kindly given
me to reproduce in this book portions of articles
which I wrote for that paper.

E. F. K.

CONTENTS

RHODESIA OF TO-DAY

I

I WILL commence this work by describing the present condition and the attitude of the natives in Mashonaland and Matabeleland ; for that we should secure their friendliness and obtain their labour at a moderate cost are matters of the first importance to the white settlers.

Up to this year the progress of Mashonaland has been kept back by the perpetual menace of the Matabele raids. Capitalists hesitated to invest in so dangerous a land ; it appeared a reckless venture to send valuable mining plant to the rich reefs on the ever-disturbed border. In cases where men attempted to develop their properties and put up batteries, repeated Mata-

B

bele scares would interrupt all work for weeks
or months at a time, the native labourers
deserting *en masse* to take refuge in their mountain strongholds.

But these harassing conditions exist no
longer, and there are already many signs to show
that the Matabele war has produced an excellent effect in Mashonaland. While I was at
Fort Salisbury several deputations of headmen
came in from all parts of the country to thank
Captain Duncan, as Acting Administrator, for
all the blessings which the Chartered Company's
victories had brought to their people. The
Mashonas, I found, were everywhere acting up
to their faith in our power and will to protect
them for the future against all marauders,
whether Kaffir or Portuguese. There is no longer
any difficulty in obtaining native labour for the
mines, or any risk of the work being interrupted
by the panic caused by a threatening foray. I
observed in several districts that these timid
creatures, who hitherto had dwelt in their almost
impregnable villages on the summits of the
granite *kopjies*, and who, knowing that a

Matabele raid would probably reap what they had sown, only produced a sufficiency for their immediate wants, had now actually summoned sufficient courage to descend to the fertile plains, where they are boldly building their huts in the open, and commencing to plant extensive provision gardens. They fully realise that for the future they will be able to accumulate property and enjoy a prosperity quite unknown to them before. While riding from Buluwayo to Salisbury I crossed the belt of neutral country which lies between the Matabele and the Mashonas. The former do not occupy it, and the Mashonas, before the war, were afraid to venture so near their formidable neighbours. The region was therefore left desolate, despite its rich pastures; but now I met several families of Mashonas, who, no longer fearful of Matabele raids, were migrating to this favoured portion of the High Veldt. Dr. Jameson, who was with me, conversed with some of these people, approved of their enterprise, and urged them to advise their friends to follow their example; for it is considered desirable, for several reasons, that the two races should intermingle on their common borderland.

In Mashonaland there is now no difficulty in obtaining a sufficiency of that cheap and efficient native labour without which the land, despite all its natural wealth, would remain a wilderness. The Mashonas have always shown themselves less disinclined to work than are the warlike Matabele, and it is already clear that the hut tax of ten shillings a year, which the Company is gradually imposing on the natives throughout both Mashonaland and Matabeleland—a very cheap price to pay for the protection they now enjoy—will not only in time produce a considerable revenue, but is also securing to the settlers a more important advantage. The Mashonas, like all Kaffirs—an avaricious people, unwilling to part with money or cattle—are volunteering to supply their labour to the white man in lieu of paying the tax, and are flocking to the Beira railway construction, the mines and the townships, with this object. Even the lazy Matabele warrior, who of old, after he had earned enough to buy a sufficiency of wives,

would work no more all his life through, has
found the hut tax a stimulus to exertion. Each
kraal will now supply a certain amount of
annual labour ; the natives will thus be brought
into contact with the white men and become
accustomed to the idea of working for hire. It
is found that those who come in to do a month's
work, to earn their hut tax, often remain six.
Their wants, simple now, will increase as their
civilisation advances, and it will be necessary
for them to work all the more in order to satisfy
those wants. I need scarcely say that strong
drink will not be one of those wants ; the law
that prohibits the supply of spirit to natives is
most rigidly enforced, and is not a mere dead
letter as it is in Portuguese South Africa and in
most parts of the Transvaal. I may also mention that there has recently been a great general
improvement in the attitude of the Mashonas
towards the whites. In the early days of the
Company, treated with a too great forbearance,
these ignorant savages, despising us as weak and
timorous, were insolent, often aggressive, and
pilfered from the settlers on every possible

occasion. This is no longer the case ; now the Company's police promptly visit the kraal of the offenders to punish or obtain compensation, while the Matabele war has taught the Mashonas that the white men are people to be respected.

In Mashonaland, therefore, the native question presents few difficulties, while in Matabeleland, also, it has now been practically settled with an ease that astonished all beholders. Those who were not in the country at the time can scarcely realise the extraordinary rapidity with which this region of turbulent savages, this last stronghold of South African barbarism, has been completely pacified. Absolute security to life and property was the immediate result of the successful campaign which broke up the Matabele military system, and very great credit indeed is due to the Administrator and other officers of the Chartered Company, who have with such admirable tact, discretion and decision brought about this end.

The war was scarcely over when I reached Buluwayo in January. The king and his broken impis were still on the Shangani, none of the important indunas had come in, and yet I found a Civil Government in Buluwayo with its machinery in full working order, administering and settling the country without fuss or trouble. It was as if no war had ever been; the white men—a most orderly community for a new country—having fought throughout the campaign, had now laid aside their arms and settled down to their respective occupations. A mere handful of police patrolled the country and maintained order among the natives; prospectors in pairs or singly were wandering over the land in all directions, and, far from being molested, were well received by the natives, whether Matabele or Amaholi. This was my own experience when I walked unarmed, with two Matabele to carry my baggage, early in February, over the hilly country near the Mavin military kraal, one hundred miles north-east of Buluwayo. On several occasions I met prospectors, disbanded volunteers of the expedition, living on the happiest terms with the men they had so recently been fighting. I soon discovered that the inhabitants of Matabeleland are not a

difficult people to deal with. Suspicious though
they are by nature, they evidently trust the
white men implicitly, and I am happy to say
that their confidence is rarely abused; it is not
indeed to the interest of prospectors and other
travellers to forfeit the good-will of these inde-
pendent Kaffirs, who know how to boycott those
who offend them, and if ill-treated would ob-
stinately refuse to supply necessaries, despite
threats or offers of cloth unlimited.

The natives appeared to be unaffectedly
pleased to see the white man in their country,
and there is no doubt that our invasion and
occupation have been welcomed by the vast
bulk of the Matabele nation, which consists of a
peaceable people of mixed breed, descendants of
captive women taken in various raids, men compelled to fight by their rulers, cruel at the
bidding of their king, but naturally having no
relish for war or bloodshed—in short, a mild,
pastoral race that, so soon as the barbarous
system that ground them down was destroyed,
became quite reconciled to the new condition of
things. One class alone may still resent our

rule, a small minority, however, which is never likely to show fight again—the military caste of the young Majakas, who were ever eager for war and anxious to maintain the blood-thirsty old Zulu traditions, the murderous raiders on the helpless Mashonas, who will no longer be permitted to indulge in their atrocious sport, but whom the Company's officers will soon convert into excellent native police and soldiery.

Later on, when the Administrator, Dr. Jameson, had received all the chief Matabele indunas on their 'coming in,' and had fully explained to them what the position of the natives would be under the new régime, the pacification and contentment of the people was still more fully assured. For then they learnt that the white men had no intention of despoiling or punishing them, and the indunas discovered to their joy that, far from being degraded from their former rank, they were to rule their people exactly as of old, save that they would not be entrusted with the power of life and death, the prerogative of the white indunas, and would be punished if they acted with cruelty or injustice towards those placed under them ; the Matabele indunas would be responsible to the white men for the conduct of their people, and the white magistrates would support their authority in their kraals if necessary. Such support was indeed given on several occasions while I was in the country ; for in that time in some of the outlying districts individual Matabele—unruly Majakas or recently enfranchised Amaholi slaves no longer afraid of their vanquished and disarmed masters—availing themselves of the interregnum between the overthrow of the king's rule and the complete establishment of the Company's Government, were behaving in a lawless manner, lifting the cattle of their neighbours, interfering with their women, and committing other offences. These cases were tried by white inspectors of police, with native indunas sitting as assessors, and, if found guilty the offenders were fined a few head of cattle, flogged, or summarily executed, according to the gravity of their crime. It is a sufficient proof of the native confidence in the justice of the white man that quite recently Gambo, Secombo, and eight other head indunas interviewed Dr. Jameson and requested him to place a white policeman in each of their districts, who should strengthen their authority, and to whom they could appeal in the event of disputes among themselves. This partial restoration of their former power to the Matabele chieftains, who will now compose a native magistracy under our control, has greatly facilitated the administration of the country. This system is satisfactory to the natives, and, under the circumstances, it appears to be the only one that could have been adopted.

It has also been explained to the indunas that the disarmament of the Matabele—which was only partial—is but a temporary measure, and that when the country is settled the weapons necessary for purposes of hunting and defence against wild animals will be returned to them. They also now fully understand that the white men have no intention of interfering with the laws and customs of the Matabele, save that there must be no more raiding, no more murder,

and no more witchcraft. The practice of witchcraft is being rigorously suppressed, to the
disgust of the witch-doctors themselves, whose
profitable occupation is gone, and to the manifest delight, tempered with superstitious dread,
of the people. These witch-doctors exert an
immense influence, always for evil, over the
minds of these savages; horrible cruelties and
all manner of crimes have been perpetrated by
them. Witchcraft, as practised here, is invariably the prelude to murder, and should be
stamped out as completely as Obeah has been
in most of the West Indian Islands. Till now
no man dared acquire wealth, or appear richer
than his neighbours, for some envious witch-
doctor would be sure to smell him out as a
witch; he would undergo a mock trial, be found
guilty, and then himself, every member of his
family, and even his dogs, would be slaughtered,
while all his property would be confiscated, to
be divided between the king, the witch-doctor,
and the judges. Protected as they now are
against this horrible system, it is not to be won-
dered at that the natives have accepted our

rule with readiness. There were many other oppressive customs besides that of witchcraft which formerly prevented a man from ever attaining any degree of wealth or comfort. Everything in the country was practically the king's property, his the cattle, his the proceeds of the raids. Those of his subjects who went to Tati or to Kimberley, to work in the mines of the white men, forfeited the greater portion of their savings on their return to their own country, for they were compelled under penalty of death to make what was by courtesy called a present of considerable value to Lobengula.

Before the war the people owned but a very small proportion of the cattle; an important induna would only possess a dozen head or so. Since the war they have not only been assigned a sufficiency of cattle for all their needs, but they have undoubtedly appropriated a great number of the royal cattle, falsely asserting that these were their individual property. The Chartered Company, as the successor of Lobengula, lays claim to all the goods of the late king; but it will of course not be feasible to enforce a restitution of all the cattle that have been 'jumped' by the natives, and the Matabele will probably now be far richer in cattle than they ever were before. Any rights the people may have possessed to the use of the king's vast herds they still possess in full. Instead of taking charge of these cattle for the king, they now do so for the Chartered Company, and have the use of the milk as they had formerly.

The sudden pacification of Matabeleland is thus easily explained. The people realise that they can cultivate their lands and acquire cattle without fear of the witch-doctor's eye and Lobengula's murderous greed. Of magnificent pasture on the High Veldt there is practically an unlimited supply ; the natives never made use of a tithe of it ; there is ample room for both black and white on those healthy uplands. The Matabele have been told that they can return to those portions of the High Veldt which they occupied before the war, there to cultivate their gardens and look after their cattle as of old, save where circumstances render a different course advisable. Thus kraals situated amid extensive auriferous reefs, likely to attract numbers of white prospectors, or upon sites of proposed townships or other public works, will have to be removed ; but in all cases the natives will be assigned lands as favourable for grazing and agricultural pur- poses as those they have been asked to sur- render. As it is the universal custom of the Kaffirs to destroy their kraals after having occupied them for some years, and to remove to other locations, this enforced migration, which after all will only be necessary in a limited number of cases, forms no real grievance, and at no indaba at which I was present did a single chief raise any objection on this score.

The policy, therefore, which has been adopted by the Company, and which commends itself to all on the spot, is to leave the Matabele kraals so far as is possible where they were. They will thus be scattered among the farms of the white men, as in Mashonaland, where the system is working well; native labour will be readily procurable, the Kaffirs will soon attain such civilisation as is possible to them, and

moreover, they will be under our immediate
supervision.   It is well that the system of
forming large native reserves, which has been
found so disastrous in other portions of South
Africa, has not been adopted in Matabeleland.
To set these savages apart in reserves would be
to indefinitely retard their civilisation.   Rich
in cattle and mealie crops they would refuse to
labour for us, and would pass their lives in
indolence; they would be outside our control,
and consequently murder and witchcraft would
flourish as of old; while, gathered together in
numbers at their periodical beer drinkings, the
young men would talk big, scheme for war, and
hatch all manner of mischief.

It is, of course, the aim of the Chartered
Company to procure a plentiful supply of native
labour, and the only method of insuring this is
to give the Matabele who come in to work kind
and fair treatment and honest wage.   It is
totally untrue that (as has been recently
stated) compulsion or threats have been employed; such a system would defeat its own
object, for there would be nothing to prevent

the men running away. The responsible indunas have been told that if the young men in their respective districts choose to work for the white men in the mines, the fields, or the townships, they will have good food and will be guaranteed a minimum wage of ten shillings a month. Every inducement is held out to them to supply their voluntary labour, and not without satisfactory result. They quite realise that the white Government is determined to do them justice. In the few instances in which individual prospectors or other white men have attempted to force the natives to work, or have otherwise ill-treated them, the offenders have been severely punished, and when I was in Buluwayo two or three white men were confined in goal on this account. At the end of last July 800 Matabele came into Buluwayo to work on the brickfields and in other capacities. Of these the majority are still there, having voluntarily entered into a further engagement at the end of each month, which is a sufficient proof that they are not ill-used.

It is to be hoped that they will not become

C

even too well off, and wax fat, lazy, and useless, they and their cattle multiplying in peace, all their wants being supplied with a minimum of labour—as is the case in Bechuanaland, where the native is in enjoyment of every comfort he can appreciate, and is prosperous even from a European standpoint, his lot being undoubtedly far preferable to that of the bulk of the peasantry in Great Britain. It will probably be found advisable to establish an official scale of pay for native labour in Matabeleland, so as to obviate that rapid and quite unnecessary rise in the rate of wages which has occurred in other parts of South Africa, to the detriment of European enterprise, without being in the least degree conducive to the real welfare of the Kaffir.

Some of the old traders in Matabeleland, jealous of the Chartered Company's intrusion into what they looked upon as their own preserve, profess to be of opinion that the Company is making the mistake of treating the natives altogether too kindly, that this clemency will be considered a sign of weakness and cowardice on the part of the white man. I cannot agree with this view. I do not believe the Company's clemency is misunderstood at all. I was present at all the indabas or official interviews between Dr. Jameson and the principal Matabele leaders at the close of the war. On first presenting themselves the chiefs looked downcast, and waited with forebodings to hear the 'Great White Chief's' will; but, at the end of the interview, when they understood how the Matabele were to be treated by their conquerors, their minds were evidently much relieved. 'Now we can go away and sleep,' they used to say—the Matabele way of conveying that one's fears have been set at rest. To all appearance they were sincerely grateful, and were quite in earnest when they said that they had no grievance against the white men, and for the future would be our friends. The gallant stand of Wilson and his men, who, as old Umjan, who led the attack upon them, admiringly said, 'fell fighting together in a ring, men of men, whose fathers were men before them,' has quite dispelled any idea the

Matabele may have held as to the timidity of the white settlers. Wilson's party did not fall in vain ; the story of the Shangani will be told in many a kraal throughout South Africa, and will go far to check the ardour of turbulent tribes, and preserve peace throughout the vast regions we control. No conquered people were ever treated with more consideration, but it will not injure our prestige to have exercised a generous leniency. Dr. Jameson declared to the assembled indunas that it was the Company's earnest wish that the white men should live in friendship with the black, and as Administrator he has certainly done his utmost, and apparently with complete success, to bring about this consummation.

II

THE CLIMATE

In Matabeleland and Mashonaland the heavy
rains fall in the summer months of December,
January, February, and March. During the dry
season, when the rainfall is but slight, the
climate seemed to me to be as delicious as any I
had ever experienced. One who travels across
the Matabele or Mashona Highlands in the
winter months has cold nights and heavy dews
for his bivouacs ; but by day he rides or walks
like the old Athenians, 'through most pellucid
air,' with generally a keen health-giving breeze
blowing and a cloudless sky overhead.

Even in the rainy summer months the
climate is not unpleasant, neither is it seriously
unhealthy. I never found the heat oppressive.
There is nearly always a fresh wind ; the down-
pour is seldom continuous, and when between

the showers the sun shines out of the rift of
blue sky and glorifies the rich tints of the
sodden, flower-spangled vegetation, the aspect
of the country is peculiarly charming, while the
air, purified and cooled by the rain, is balmy
and even bracing.   I found it difficult to realise
here that I was within the tropics; it was possible to march with comfort under the Matabele
sun in midsummer.   But it is a somewhat trying
season, nevertheless ; for the swollen rivers and
deep sloughs cut off communication and interrupt all work for weeks at a time, and it is then
that the settler, having no employment, is apt
to wax restless and discontented, airs his divers
grievances at agitation meetings, and perhaps fre-
quents the canteens more than is good for him.

Mashonaland has earned an unenviable and
undeserved reputation for unhealthiness.   It is
somewhat hotter in that country than in Matabeleland, and it appears that malaria is more
prevalent, which is no doubt partly due to the
fact that there are fewer cattle in the country ;
the grass has not been eaten down, the pasture
is not 'tame' as on the Matabele High Veldt, but

rank and high—twelve feet in height and more in the lowlands—and when rotting away after the rains is naturally productive of fever. But the malaria of both territories, I was assured by the medical men resident in the country, and I could observe the fact myself, is of a very mild type when compared to the fevers of any other tropical country, and when serious complications follow an attack these are generally due to irregularity of living on the part of the patient. Men die of whisky, and their friends charitably call it fever. Among the pioneers of a new country are to be found many men whose temperament would lead them to an early grave in whatever clime they lived, restless, dissipated men of broken fortunes and shattered constitutions, ever ready to fly to the bottle (a very poisonous bottle in Rhodesia) as the one relie to the monotony of their existence. It is not fair to judge the climate of a new country by the death rate of its first settlers.

While travelling in the rainy season I have met prospectors, far away from the nearest white settlement, making weary marches across

the swampy wilderness, ill-fed, wet through for
weeks ; and these men, whenever they reached
a camp, sick and debilitated by privation, would
promptly indulge in a three or four days 'burst'
on vilest whisky.   The hardships that were
undergone by the members of the pioneer
expedition are now historical, and few of those
men would be now alive were the malaria of a
really virulent nature.   In what country in the
world could men live with impunity the lives
they led ?   To bivouac for weeks on the rain-
swept veldt, provided with insufficient clothing,
often with insufficient food and that of bad
quality, the comforts and even necessaries of
life being absent—such has been the experience
of every pioneer and trooper in the country.   It
is obvious that such conditions must predispose
to fever and dysentery.

Of the men who took part in the recent
campaign, the troopers of the Shangani patrol
more especially endured great privations, and
this too in the rainy season and in the most
unhealthy lowlands of the whole country.   The
surgeon of the Bechuanaland Border Police

Bulawayo in the mid-1890s. Top: 1894, before the township was moved some three miles to its present site. Centre: Abercorn Street, 1895. Bottom: the Bank of Africa 'in Bulawayo.

Market Square, Bulawayo

informed me that not one of these troopers had died of fever or of any disease that could be put down to climatic influence. I was with these men at Inyati camp a month or so after their return from that disastrous patrol; they looked as healthy and as hard a body of men as one could wish to see.

I myself marched in the heart of the rains through the unhealthy district of Mavin. I rode from Buluwayo to Salisbury, 300 miles, at the most sickly season of the year, that which immediately follows the last autumnal rains, when, in places, the subsiding waters leave behind them leagues of putrifying mud and rotting vegetation. I walked through the low-lands of Portuguese Gazaland to reach the terminus of the Beira railway, and made several other journeys in different portions of the country, sleeping out on the open veldt nearly every night, in rain or soaking dew; and I can honestly say that I never enjoyed better health in my life, while the white men who accompanied me on some of these journeys were not one whit the worse for the exposure.

The High Veldt is undoubtedly healthy in both territories. Buluwayo itself, for example, appears to be entirely free from malaria, for I did not hear of a single case of fever that had been acquired in the township or in its neighbourhood. That the Low Veldt is malarious during the rainy season is a matter of no great consequence, for, so far as is yet known, there is nothing to attract the white man to that region ; the auriferous reefs, the lands adapted for farming, are on the High Veldt, and it is also along the High Veldt that the principal roads of the country are carried.

In short, this is a ' white man's country ' so far as the climate is concerned ; there is no fever here that should stay the intending British emigrant, and be it remembered, moreover, that fever appears to be the one disease he has to dread, for one hears nothing here of the influenzas, the consumptions, the rheumatics, of Old England. What fever there is will gradually disappear before occupation and civilisation, as it has done in many unhealthy districts of the Transvaal and the Cape Colony. Those who knew

the Diamond Fields and the Randt Goldfields
in the early days will remember their fevers and
their high death rate ; and yet things have so
completely changed within a few years, that these
districts are now actually frequented as health
resorts. Some forty white men, traders and
missionaries, most of whom I met, have been
living in Matabeleland for a number of years.
They all appear to enjoy good health, and their
complexions are as a rule of that ruddy hue
which is quite incompatible with the malarial
diathesis. The few white children that have
been born in the country are also as rosy of
cheek and as sturdy of limb as if they had been
reared in England. As for Mashonaland, several
writers have exaggerated the evils of the climate,
or have at any rate described a state of things
that no longer exists or is passing away. With
increased facilities of communication, the privations that had to be endured by the early settlers
can be avoided. So soon as the white population
is properly housed and properly nourished, this
region for salubrity ought to compare favourably with any of our colonies.

III

GRAZING AND AGRICULTURE

THE traveller who has reached Matabeleland by way of the dreary Bechuanaland plains can readily understand how it is that Lobengula's father and his people, when driven from Marico, trekked 500 miles to the northward before they settled again—there is no such good land between. The extraordinary richness of the soil in both Matabeleland and Mashonaland is at once revealed by the luxuriance of the vegetation. The first glimpse of Matabeleland, as one emerges from the pass beyond Mangwe, on the northern road, is particularly pleasing, and gives one a fair idea of the general character of the High Veldt. As I saw it in early morning, it was as delicious a scene as could well be imagined. From the ridge on which I stood I could see far over the country; isolated granite *kopjies* of curious formation, generally well wooded or covered with flowering bushes, and crowned at the top with great rocks, shaped like ruined castles, were scattered over the undulating veldt, across which wound many streams of clear water, flowing over sandy beds ; ranges of wooded hills hemmed in amphitheatres of rich pasture full of a variety of beautiful flowers, the haunts of birds and gorgeous butterflies.

When one has travelled day after day across the flowery veldt, finding at certain seasons of the year a profusion of delicious wild fruits of many varieties, with which one could sustain life if one were lost ; when one beholds the magnificent crops which reward the lazy Kaffir for a mere scratching of the soil, but a soil inexhaustibly rich, replenished as it is each rainy season by the matter washed down from the disintegrating granite of the *kopjies*, one realises that the title of the Promised Land was not altogether wrongly bestowed on this fair region. I will now attempt to show what the conditions of farming will be (*a*) in Matabeleland and (*b*) in Mashonaland.

(a) In Matabeleland.

That a great portion of the Matabele High
Veldt is admirably adapted for farming there
can be no doubt. The best districts are, of
course, those in which Lobengula used to graze
his vast herds of cattle, and where the grass,
eaten down for years, has become sweet and
wholesome for cattle. Boer and Colonial farmers
who have come into this country speak enthu-
siastically of its possibilities.

A large number of farms have already been
pegged out. Of these some 700 are ' volunteer
farms,' which were granted free to the men who
took part in the late expedition. Each volunteer farm is of 3,000 morgen (6,000 acres),
carrying with it a nominal annual quit rent of
ten shillings. These farms are transferable, and
are now to be bought at from 45*l.* to 150*l.*
Farming rights, entitling the holder to peg out
3,000 acres, can also be bought directly from the
Company at eighteenpence an acre ; but in the
case of these farms a *bonâ fide* occupation must

be effected within a reasonable time—a condition not attached to the holding of a volunteer farm. The Company, in thus refusing to sell its land under what it considers a fair value, irrespective of the present quotation of the volunteer farms, and in adding the occupation condition, is carrying out its promises made before the war to the volunteers, who very properly are to have the first chance in the new country. The measure will also prevent the land being bought up at this early stage by large syndicates for purely speculative purposes.

While riding from Buluwayo to Salisbury, following the route by which the Salisbury Column had entered Matabeleland, and so passing the Shangani and Bembezi battle-fields, I traversed what is, perhaps, the finest portion of the Matabele High Veldt for a distance of some 250 miles. This route is carried along the watershed between the rivers flowing eastward into the Crocodile and Sabi, and those flowing westward to the Zambesi. I rode day after day through the keen bracing air, under a blue sky, across a magnificent country, undulating pasture diversified with groves of various trees and bushes, and watered by a multitude of clear streams; even in the driest seasons there is no lack of water, and, indeed, there are few regions in the world so well watered as Matabeleland and Mashonaland. From high ridges we often overlooked vast landscapes, the dark summits of the Matoppo Hills and other ranges closing the horizon to the east. It would be difficult to find anywhere a country better adapted for farming than the High Veldt of the great watershed, which covers an immense area. The climate is excellent; there is ample room for a great number of immigrants, for this region appears to be but sparsely occupied by the natives, though it abounds in wild animals; the now somewhat rare black wildebeeste is to be found here, and lions are numerous in some parts.

Even though gold prospects prove deceptive, and the consequent absence of a local market checks farming enterprise for the present, the pressure of population in Europe must ultimately turn the tide of emigration in this direction. Whatever may befall the Chartered

Company, it will have deserved well of Great Britain for having pegged out this rich land for her posterity. The contour of the country in many places offers facilities for artificial irrigation during the winter droughts, so that the rich soil could readily be made to yield abundant summer crops, as in the Transvaal; and the day must come when this verdant wilderness, with its infinite possibilities, this breezy highland tract of broad vales, gently sloping hills and limpid streams, will gladden the traveller's eyes with pleasant homesteads, orchards, and waving cornfields, as do at present the happy valleys of Marico, the home of the Matabele sixty years ago.

But we may not have to wait long for the change. The principal gold belt of the country extends from end to end of this watershed. A large mining population is likely to soon afford a market for the farmer's produce. The Gwailo goldfield, the most promising in Matabeleland, of which I shall have to speak later on, is in the centre of this doubly-favoured region. The Gwailo township will soon be a considerable place. When I passed through it the township

D

consisted of one mud, thatched hut—the post-office and hotel combined; but since then a number of stands have been purchased from the Company, and building is rapidly progressing. The mineral wealth of the district is attracting hundreds of white men; syndicates, companies and individuals have pegged out a number of farms, one syndicate alone possessing a magnificent estate of 80,000 acres. There are other districts as well adapted for farming as the Crocodile-Zambesi watershed, and in all directions around Buluwayo itself rich pasture and land capable of irrigated cultivation is to be found.

An intending farmer will, of course, realise that for some time he will have to contend with difficulty of communication, and distance from an adequate market. But he can at present purchase the best of grazing or arable land at a trifling price, and should the gold reefs answer the expectations now held by even cautious miners, and more especially should an alluvial goldfield of any extent be discovered, the value of land will of course greatly increase. As for other drawbacks, it does not appear that locusts work more mischief here than they do in other portions of South Africa. Lung sickness among the cattle is not more prevalent than in the Transvaal, and inoculation for this disease has proved quite successful. The principal curse of the country is the devastating horse sickness, for which no remedy has yet been discovered, so that salted horses (those that have recovered from the sickness and have immunity for the future) are very expensive; but this disease will no doubt die out as the country becomes occupied, even as it has already done in districts further south.

(b) IN MASHONALAND.

Special farming rights were granted to members of the old Pioneer Force in Mashonaland. These, like the volunteer rights in Matabeleland, entitle the owner to peg out a farm free of any conditions as to *bonâ fide* occupation. These pioneer farms are of 3,000 acres each, not of 6,000 as in the case of the volunteer farms, and

carry an annual quit rent of 1*l*. About 190 of
these rights were issued, and some are occa-
sionally offered for sale at from 50*l*. to 60*l*. ; a
located farm is of course much more valuable
than a right.

These rights are undoubtedly very cheap at
this price, when it is considered that Mashonaland has had three years' start of Matabeleland,
that more is consequently known about its possibilities, and that its ultimate prosperity is a
matter of greater certainty. There is no reason
for coming to the conclusion that it is not in
all respects as good a country as Matabeleland.
There has been a tendency of late to boom
Matabeleland at the expense of the first settled
territory, and a considerable depression has set
in in Mashonaland. But this will not last long ;
the fortunes of Matabeleland and Mashonaland
are so intimately linked that the two cannot but
advance together. When I was in Mashonaland
the townships were half deserted—there had
been a diversion of population and capital to
Matabeleland ; but those who remained realised
that this was but a temporary evil, and that

when the first wild rush to the new country had spent itself, one territory would participate in the prosperity of the other. The development of Mashonaland has been delayed by various causes, the principal of which have been lack of capital, difficulty of communication (and hence an extravagantly high scale of prices for all commodities), and the scare of Matabele raids. Capital is at last flowing in; the Beira railway is rapidly progressing; and the last-mentioned evil has been removed for ever. There is every sign to show that Mashonaland will now attain prosperity by rapid strides. It is very unfortunate, however, that the long stagnation crushed many of the smaller men, who could not afford to wait the turn of the tide, but were compelled to sell their properties at depreciated prices; and among these men were some of the pick of the country—the original pioneers who won Mashonaland.

In the last official report of the Chartered Company on agricultural and stock-farming prospects in Mashonaland, it is shown that but little has been done so far, but that what little has been attempted fully proves the great capacities of the country. Even in districts where the soil is sandy and comparatively poor, the natives produce good crops. Wheat, rice, forage, mealies, tobacco, and all the fruits and vegetables of Europe and the sub-tropics do well here. Dairy farming and market gardening near the townships prove very remunerative, but at present these industries are mainly in the hands of the East Indian coolies. Tobacco can be cultivated nearly everywhere, and is grown in all the native kraals. Sugar, coffee, and other tropical produce thrive in some districts. Indeed, Mashonaland appears to be better fitted for agriculture than Matabeleland ; but the latter country is, and will be for some years to come, more favourable for stock-farming, the grass, as I have already explained, having been eaten down for forty years by the vast herds of the king's cattle, and rendered ' tame.' Many of the king's cattle are now being brought into Mashonaland ; they show a good strain of blood, and his sheep, too, are often of good stock.

Wherever I travelled in Mashonaland I found

the country well watered and the soil rich. I visited most of the few real farms that at present exist. Most of the so-called farmers are merely prospectors and storekeepers, who have done next to no work on their land. Among other farms I visited that of Morgen Ster, a mission station of the Dutch Reformed Church, which is about three miles from the extraordinary ruins of Zimbabwe. Here the missionaries have provided visible proof of the richness of the soil and of the farming possibilities of the land by bringing under cultivation an extensive tract, from which they supply the township of Victoria with vegetables and other produce. On the long irrigated terraces of red soil the bananas and other fruit trees of the tropics grow side by side with the figs, peaches, apples, and vines of Europe, while all the vegetables of England thrive on these fertile acres. Near Salisbury, also, similar and equally successful farms are to be found.

But what appeared to me to be the pick of the country from the agricultural point of view is the beautiful district of Manica. Leaving the township of Umtali I walked over the Manica gold belt, which extends from west to east along the ranges of the Manica mountains. My way lay along the summits of the breezy ridges, and I looked down upon fertile valleys in whose hollows nestled the kraals and gardens of the Kaffirs. Here and there, too, near the shafts and adits of the mines, were the houses of managers and prospectors, each surrounded by its carefully irrigated garden, where pumpkins, cauliflowers, potatoes, carrots, tomatoes, gooseberries, currants—in short, all the fruits and vegetables of England—flourished and attained a size that would have gladdened the heart of a British gardener. Manica is the garden of this portion of Africa. Almost anything would grow here. The oranges and other fruits are delicious. In these warm valleys the soil is often forty feet in depth, and is well suited for the cultivation of tropical produce. Plantations of coffee, sugar, and tea would probably prove remunerative. There is fine timber on the hills, and the bark of one species of tree is employed for tanning, while indiarubber grows wild in

Knight's mode of transport: a Zeederberg coach

The hazards of pioneer travel

A mine battery at Hartley Hills in the early 1890s.

Lobengula's old five-stamp battery at Pomposo mine

the lowlands. I may mention incidentally that poultry—the main diet of the European traveller —are free from the diseases which play havoc with them in other parts of the country.

This district enjoys one inestimable advantage over the rest of Rhodesia—the Beira railway is already close to Manica and will shortly pass through the heart of it, affording cheap and rapid communication to the East Coast. It is this fact which renders a scheme, which was suggested to me by one who has carefully studied the subject, appear feasible. In Manica the dry and rainy seasons are not so sharply defined as in Matabeleland and Western Mashonaland. It is true that here, too, in winter the grass dries up in the valleys and on the lower slopes of the hills; but on the ridges and domed summits of these mountains, from five to six thousand feet above the sea, light rains fall even in the heart of winter, so that the grass remains green, and is generally short and sweet, affording the best of pasture. It was pointed out to me that scientific dairy farming, now so profitably carried on in Victoria and other portions

of Australia, ought to prove equally successful
here. From the grazing grounds of Victoria,
which, unlike these, have to be irrigated at
considerable expense, quantities of butter are
exported annually to England. An association
of small farmers from England might do something of the same sort here so soon as the Beira
railway reaches the district. A hundred head
of cattle would probably go to a 300 morgen
highland farm. The milk could be carried
down from the farms by the natives—they are
hereditary carriers—to some central factory near
the railway, there to be converted into butter for
the home market. This scheme appears practicable; but unfortunately that portion of the
Manica Highlands which is perhaps the best
adapted for grazing purposes has been declared
a goldfield by the British South Africa Company,
and is therefore practically closed to farmers
according to the Company's present law.

It will be remembered that the eastern
frontier of Manica has not yet been wholly
demarcated. After following the gold belt for
some ten miles I reached the summit of one

of the highest peaks of the country, known as the Crow's Nest, from which I overlooked an immense and magnificent landscape extending far into Portuguese Gazaland. This peak is on the divide—the watershed between the Umtali and Revue rivers—which the Portuguese claim as their frontier; but the Chartered Company maintains that the undulating country between this divide and the Chua Hills, several leagues further east, forms part of its territory. From where I stood I could see the whole of this debatable land stretching out before me, a land of rolling downs, wooded mountains and rugged peaks, a land known to be rich in gold and other minerals, and whose valleys, into which the streams dash in cascades from many ravines, are of exceeding fertility, planted with native gardens of bananas and other tropical fruits. The possession of this debatable belt is still a point of issue between ourselves and the Portuguese (whose title, from what I gather, is shadowy in the extreme). We should certainly not lightly abandon so rich a district if we can show our right to it.

IV

EMIGRATION TO MATABELELAND

DISTANT and difficult of communication as is
Matabeleland, and expensive as is the journey,
the rush of adventurers thither commenced even
before the war had been brought to a close.
Last April the white population of Buluwayo
itself numbered about 250 ; but in August there
were some 3,000 Europeans in the township
and the immediate vicinity.   When I was there
the community certainly seemed a remarkably
orderly one, when it is remembered that this
was then but the rough camp of a ' new rush ; '
there were few black sheep, the majority being
respectable men, each intent on pushing his own
particular business.   In fact, at that time the
people who were entering the country were
mostly of the right stamp ; it made one feel
proud of one's race to look at the crowd of

some 500 men—of the fair sex only one—which attended the gymkana meeting at Buluwayo on Easter Monday. Energetic, stalwart, bronzed, keen of eye, these pioneers of Matabeleland were the very pick of Anglo-Saxon manhood. The Company has wisely restricted the issue of canteen licenses to a few well-known and responsible traders, and there is little of that drunken rowdiness generally associated with a rush of miners and adventurers to a new country. Crimes of violence have always been singularly rare on the gold and diamond diggings of South Africa. The revolver and the knife of old California are not tolerated, and lynching is unknown. But at Buluwayo, as elsewhere in South Africa, the ancient British method of settling a dispute is a recognised institution, and you will not uncommonly see two prospectors or others who have come in ' on the spree ' having it out in a few rounds outside the canteen in orthodox style. I have never come across a community more free from brutality, fonder of fair play, and more manly than that of the temporary camp of Buluwayo a few months back. One lived in a healthier moral atmosphere than one does in most parts of the world.

All these people seemed sanguine of the country's future, and they gave a substantial proof of their confidence by investing considerable sums in farms, mining rights, stands and other securities. I was present at the auction of the first 100 stands, or township building lots, in Buluwayo, which took place on March 24. The upset price of a stand was fixed at 30*l.*; all were sold, at an average price of 50*l.*; in some cases keen competition for stands in the marketplace raised the bidding to 160*l.*; and this despite the onerous conditions of sale, for, unless the purchaser of a stand had within three months erected upon it a substantial building of iron or stone of the value of 200*l.*, he forfeited his stand and the deposit he had paid; moreover, at that time, pending the settlement of the country, the Chartered Company was unable to give a valid title to a stand-owner and refused to register any transfer to a third party, the result being that speculative buyers were kept out and the bidding was confined to *bonâ fide* purchasers, men who intend to remain in Matabeleland and take a part in its development.

That those in the country are not losing faith in its prospects is shown by the marvellous result of the last sale of stands in Buluwayo, held on July 31 and August 1. Forty-five lots alone realised 9,207*l*. Ten lots were sold at over 400*l*. a piece ; one fetched 900*l*. 36,530*l*. was realised by the Company in these two days, and in all it has received about 50,000*l*. by the sale of stands in Buluwayo and Gwailo since the occupation. On these stands costly buildings are rapidly rising. The Standard and other Cape banks, having evidently come to the conclusion that Buluwayo's prosperity is not a mere bubble boom, are expending large sums on permanent offices. The Government Buildings are now in hand, and one hotel alone is being erected at a cost of 5,000*l*. By the end of July about 50,000*l*. had been laid out in building.

On April 25, Matabeleland was thrown open to the world ; those who took part in the cam-

paign having already secured their promised
award of land or reef, all others who choose are
now at liberty to come into the country and peg
out their claims. So now the adventurers are
flocking in their hundreds and thousands into
Matabeleland, numbers deserting the Randt and
Mashonaland for the purpose, all eager to try
their luck in the land of gold. Most of these
are settlers of the right sort, but numbers, of
course, are the very reverse. This is no country
for the ' waster,' the man of no trade and no
means. Men of this class, arriving penniless,
not being able to turn their hands to any work,
soon fall on the charity of the Chartered Company, which here, as of old in Mashonaland, has
had to issue free rations to the indigent, a
generosity which has been much abused. The
man who can work, and honestly intends to
work, will in many cases be assisted until he
can obtain employment ; but the ' waster ' will
be compelled to wend his way back to the south
as fast as he is able.

Just now ignorant people at home appear to
imagine that they only have to land in South

Africa to find a fortune lying at their feet ready
to be picked up. Numbers of English clerks
and others, accustomed to a town life, have
contrived to reach Matabeleland, only to be
bitterly disappointed, for it is no country for
such as they, and every step should be taken to
prevent these poor fellows from crossing the
ocean, leaving possibly a small competence, to
encounter almost certain failure, misery, and
often death. Strangely infatuated indeed were
some of the men I met tramping up the road to
the Promised Land, veritable Micawbers, confident that something must turn up to their
benefit in such a golden realm. On reaching
Buluwayo they found that there was no work
which they could do, and that all the necessaries
of life were at nearly famine prices, so they soon
exhausted their resources. Many even arrived
with insufficient clothing and bedding to shelter
them during the winter, and the Company has
found it necessary to issue a notice warning
immigrants to provide themselves with these
necessaries before entering the country. Some
of the poor wretches never even behold the land

E

of their desire, but perish of fever or privation while tramping up the long road from the south, through the wilds of Bechuanaland. Shortly before I left Buluwayo a young Scotchman, who had come all the way from Glasgow, attracted by the tales of gold, to seek his fortune here, was found one morning lying dead under a tree just outside the camp ; he had succumbed when within a mile of the El Dorado towards which he had been struggling.

It should be clearly understood by this class that no alluvial goldfield has yet been discovered in Matabeleland, and that it is therefore no country for the individual digger of no means and no experience. It is only by the employ-ment of expensive machinery that reef workings can be made to pay in South Africa. Skilful miners from Cornwall are doing well in the mines here as managers, overseers, and in other responsible positions ; but the demand for these is limited, and the ordinary white miner is not required, as several Cornishmen, who have recently returned home disappointed, have found to their cost. For this is a black man's country; native labour is abundant, efficient (the Mashonas are hereditary miners), and so cheap that no white labour can compete with it. These elementary facts should be impressed on the minds of poor men at home who have read glowing tales of the fortunes made by diggers in Australia and California, and who imagine the conditions are the same in Africa. The white unskilled labourer can do nothing here; if he remains in the country he is likely to degrade into that shame of our race to be found in every country where native labour is procurable, the mean white, a lower creature far than the black savage by his side. The merchants at Cape Town are now overwhelmed with applications from honest and well-educated young Englishmen, victims of the South African boom, or rather of their ignorance of what it signifies, eager, starving as they are, to accept any employment, and do nigger's work at below a nigger's wage.

But Matabeleland offers a good opening to emigrants of the right sort from home; farmers and skilled artisans are wanted; the latter, of

course, have a very good chance indeed in the
new country, provided they be steady men, but
even they should not arrive in an indigent
condition.   Masons and carpenters, more especially, readily procure work at high wages just
now, for all the new townships have yet to be
built.   Expert prospectors, acting on their own
account or as agents for others, were doing very
well when I left the country, and there was room
for more.   Amateur prospectors were plentiful
enough ; a man of little or no experience in
gold mining would travel through the country,
give the natives a pound of beads or a few
yards of limbo to show him where some ancient
workings were, and then, without further examination, peg out his claim on them—with a fair
chance, it must be allowed, of hitting on auriferous quartz of high grade, for the ancient
miners who had preceded him knew what they
were about.

A young fellow with a few hundreds to risk
might do worse than spend a holiday prospecting in Matabeleland in the company of an old
hand.   The expenses of travelling, once that he

has reached the country, are small; he might gain nothing but his experience; on the other hand he might be lucky enough to strike a good thing.

Storekeepers provided with a little capital are doing very well indeed in Matabeleland, but now that competition is increasing they must not expect the exorbitant profits that have prevailed so far. Even since I left Buluwayo prices have fallen by one-half.

I have spoken of the farmer's and the planter's chances in a previous chapter, but I may repeat that market-gardening in the vicinity of a rising township is the least speculative and most profitable business that can be undertaken by a pioneer. Some suggested philanthropical schemes for sending pauper agriculturists to Matabeleland are likely to prove failures, unless they be carried out on an almost impossibly large and munificent scale, for in a black man's land the squatter will become the mean white.

Many a young fellow has gone out to a colony innocent of its ways, invested his small capital in ranch or farm, and lost it all. Had he

kept his money in the bank until he had gained
his experience he might, on the contrary, have
made a fortune. Now the Chartered Company
holds out to a stalwart youngster an opportunity of saving his money, while he is having a
good look round the country and gaining plenty
of useful experience, before he makes up his
mind what to do and settles down. To enlist in
the Company's Mounted Police for a few months
is, in my opinion, the best thing the young
fellow fresh from home or from the colony can
possibly do on his arrival in Matabeleland. His
constant patrols among the native kraals and his
other duties will teach him much. I have met
several men who have thus profited by their
service in the Company's force. The troopers
are a good lot, as a rule, a remarkable proportion of them being gentlemen, men who have
held Her Majesty's commission, public school
boys, University men and others.

I will conclude this chapter by quoting some
passages from an article I wrote before I had
seen Matabeleland itself. The article described
my visit to the former home of the Matabele,

the Marico Valley in the Transvaal. This district bears a striking resemblance to many portions of Matabeleland and Mashonaland. It is no richer a land, no better in any respect, save that it has been occupied by white men for many years, and that it has recently been brought within easy reach of the railway. The Matabele High Veldt is far healthier than was Marico before it was cleared and cultivated. I merely put it forth as a suggestion; but why should not the Metayer system, as carried out in the Transvaal and as described below, succeed on Matabeleland farms later on—and at not a very remote date, should the country progress at its present rate—and so enable young men of some experience but small means to get a start in life without risking their capital? I have also quoted my description of the aspect of the Marico Valley, as I think it would apply exactly to some settled spot in the Matabeleland of the future :—

'A Cape cart carried my companion and myself in about five hours from Mafeking across the veldt to the head waters of the Notwani river.

Our road was over a grassy plain bright with
many spring flowers, on which we saw numbers
of buck and hartebeeste.   At last we reached
the foot of a low range of hills, wound up their
slope till we attained the summit of a gap, and
from here we looked down on the broad vale of
Marico lying low beneath us.   Our descent into
this hollow land was much longer than had been
our ascent to the gap, for from Mafeking we
had been driving across the High Veldt, which is
at a greater elevation than the Marico district
by several hundred feet.   It was a magnificent
landscape that stretched before us, a rolling land
as fertile as it was beautiful.   On the hill-tops
were green groves of wild fruit trees and flowering bushes.   Undulating pastures, rich as those
of Norman valleys, sloped to the flats that
bordered the winding stream, while far off on
the horizon lay the blue hills of the Witwatersrand.   Amid the vivid green of the well-watered
pastures of the valley bottom were scattered
ruddy patches, the freshly ploughed fields—the
soil is of the same red colour as in parts of
Devon—while here and there a farmhouse with

The beginnings of Fort Victoria, 1893

The fort at Fort Victoria, constructed in 1893, forming part
of the government buildings and photographed in 1896

Fort Victoria residents, 1894

Old Umtali

its white walls and thatched roof peeped from the fresh foliage of the orchards that surrounded it. This Marico Valley, which extends for some forty miles, is known as the granary of the Transvaal, and the irrigated lands produce great quantities of grain.

'This fat land was the old home of Moselekatse, Lobengula's father. The Zulus and other warlike Kaffir tribes will occupy none but the richest country, and they will trek far to find it. Wherever these people have established their kraals one may be certain that the land is a good one. It is now forty years since the Boers from the Free State, with the assistance of Montsioa, the present chief of the Barolongs, whose principal kraal is hard by Mafeking, fell upon Moselekatse, drove his raiding warriors out of Marico, and sent them trekking north again to pastures new. Northward they travelled, murdering the unwarlike people and lifting cattle as they went, crossing hundreds of miles of good country—it is a sea of verdure for the most part, but yet not good enough to satisfy a Zulu—until at last, having wandered 450 miles as the crow flies

from Marico, they came to a region even more
favoured than that they had left, and settled
down in Matabeleland. The remains of Moselekatse's kraals are still standing in Marico. On
the summit of one isolated *kopjie*, rising from
the middle of the valley, I found what was
probably the chief stronghold of this people, a
magnificent strategical position with steep rocky
sides, difficult to storm. On the highest point
of this old kraal was a mound of stones,
evidently an outlook station; it commanded a
view over the country for a great distance in all
directions; and a fair country it looked, with
its park-like expanses of glade and knee-deep
flower-spangled grass, its irrigated fields, its
snug homesteads, and the pretty little town of
Zeerust, with its white and scarlet houses, nest-
ling among poplars and fruit trees some two
leagues down the valley.

'This smiling champaign, which but a few
years back was the stronghold of savagery in
this part of Africa, the centre of a barbarous
system of organised pillage and murder, that
made of the surrounding country a wilderness

in which no man dare till the soil, now supports
numbers of prosperous white farmers and also
thousands of peaceable Kaffirs, who, freed from
the terror of the old Zulu raids, live in safety on
their lands, their cattle multiplying, the rich
soil yielding abundant crops of mealies and
Kaffir corn to the scratching of their rude
ploughs. The Marico Valley once had the
reputation of being the most unhealthy district
of the Transvaal; but, now that the farmers'
irrigation canals have drained the riverside
swamps, to carry the water to the cornfields, the
fever has almost entirely disappeared, and the
white children I saw, even in low-lying Zeerust,
looked as healthy and rosy as if they had been
bred in England. Civilisation has wrought
wonders in Marico, as it now will in Matabeleland.

'Our struggling farmers at home would be
surprised to hear of the profits which fall to
agricultural enterprise in Marico. I visited a
typical farm of the valley, the property of Mr.
H. Taylor, who, having purchased a strip of
wilderness here thirteen years ago, has gradually

converted it into a garden.   What he has done
others can do, and similar careful farming should
pay equally well in Matabeleland, as soon as a
local mining population or the extension of the
railway to Buluwayo affords a market for produce.   When I reached Mr. Taylor's solidly-
built farmhouse, with its whitewashed walls,
deep eaves, and thatched roof, I could have
imagined myself in some pretty Devon home-
stead, were it not for the tropical verandah, with
the grenadillas trained along the latticework.
There was quite an English-looking garden outside, where flourished choice roses, hollyhocks,
geraniums, stocks, and other familiar flowers.
There was a kitchen garden, too, with its straw-
berries, scarlet-runners, melons, and so forth,
while the pears, plums, figs, and other fruit
trees of England grew side by side with the
lemons, oranges, and pomegranates of a warmer
clime.   What struck me after my experience of
the slovenly ways of other colonies was that
everything on this remote South African farm,
from the dairy to the furrows of the ploughed
fields, had that trim and finished appearance we

are accustomed to at home. On going round the farm I found all hands very busy. It was harvest time; most of the grain had been brought in ; the threshing machine was hard at work, and the screw presses were packing the straw forage into compact bundles, while several waggons were loading up as rapidly as possible with both grain and forage for Buluwayo. Of this farm of 6,000 acres, 500 acres have been thoroughly cleared and are under irrigation. Three large dams store the summer floods, and from these the water furrows are carried through the fields of wheat, barley, and oats, to irrigate these winter crops during the winter droughts. The summer crops, such as maize, potatoes, and pumpkins, do not need irrigation, so portions of the property where irrigation would not be feasible are utilised for the cultivation of these.

' Mr. Taylor himself undertakes the cultivation of only a small proportion of his land. Four tenants, or rather partners—tenant is a term of too feudal a ring for democratic South Africa— work with him under a system common in the Dutch settlements, bearing a strong resemblance

to the Metayer system of certain districts in Italy.
Mr. Taylor supplies each tenant with a house, an
allotment of cleared and irrigated land, all seed
corn, and allows him the use of ploughs and
other agricultural implements. The tenant thus
practically requires no capital when he enters on
his farm ; when he has got in his harvest he has
first to return to Mr. Taylor the amount of seed
corn that was advanced to him, and then the
agricultural produce of the allotment is divided
equally between landlord and tenant. The
tenant has, of course, to keep his house in fair
repair ; he has to supply his share of labour to
maintain the dams and water furrows ; he has a
free right of pasture and fuel—both abundant—
and all profit he can make by his cattle is his
own. No written agreement is entered into
between landlord and tenant under this system.
It is understood that the former can evict when
he pleases, provided the tenant has received his
share of the year's harvest, and that the tenant
can at any moment inspan his oxen and trek off
with his belongings. This system of farming
appears to work very satisfactorily as a rule for
both parties. Many a young Englishman would

have done well if, instead of purchasing a farm on his arrival in a colony, he had first gained his experience without any risk of his capital as a Metayer tenant. I will now give two examples of what poor men can do for themselves in Marico. One of Mr. Taylor's tenants entered upon his allotment six months ago, his sole possession being a waggon and team of oxen. He has now received for his half share of the wheat and forage he has produced 450*l*. He estimates he will make 600*l*. this year, while his outgoings, for boys' wages, &c., will not exceed 100*l*. Another tenant came here five years ago, being 300*l*. in debt. He has now paid off his debt and has in all earned nearly 3,000*l*. I saw this man driving about on a Sunday in a spider trap for which he had given 120*l*. Mr. Taylor's estate also supports some hundreds of Kaffirs. They have free pasture and can clear and cultivate land for their use. In return for this they are called upon at certain seasons to weed the fields or thresh the corn. In all, they give about a month's labour in the year, receiving free rations but no pay while they are at work.'

V

THE BRITISH SOUTH AFRICA COMPANY'S MINING LAW

THE mining law in Matabeleland is identical with that in Mashonaland; but special privileges were granted to the men who took part in the recent expedition. Each volunteer had a free right to peg out twenty claims in Matabeleland at the termination of the war, and this right was transferable. For four months, from December 25 last, the volunteers had a monopoly of selection, as the Matabeleland goldfields were not thrown open to the world until April 25. Since April 25 anyone in the country is entitled to peg out a block of ten claims, a claim in both territories being 150 feet by 600 feet. The holder forfeits his block should he fail to sink a 30 feet shaft upon it within four months of registration; but if he has performed this

amount of development he can obtain another
mining right entitling him to peg out another
ten claims, and so on. When I was in the
country the Chartered Company, taking into
consideration the then lack of mining tools, was
always willing to grant extension of time to
applicants showing good cause, and in the new
laws I believe that the above conditions have
been slightly modified.[1]

Critics of the Chartered Company often
speak of it as a corporation of greedy capitalists,
whose enterprise can enrich none save them
selves and other wealthy speculators; but, as a
matter of fact, the Company is wisely doing its
best to make of this a good poor man's country.
By poor I do not mean pauper. The Company,
by putting impediments in the way of capitalist
land-grabbers, has made it possible for a man of
moderate means to have his share of the Matabeleland High Veldt, and the mining regulations
likewise compare very favourably with those of

---

[1] Concentration of development work on particular reefs is
permitted. Thus, the owner of five blocks can sink one 150 feet
shaft on one of his blocks, instead of sinking 30 feet on each of
the five blocks.

F

other countries. In order to obtain a mining right from the Company an individual must apply in person at the mining office, when he will receive his mining license entitling him to peg out his ten claims only.[1] The Company thus limits the use of licenses to men who are in the country, but the holder of a license can, of course, dispose of his rights to a third party. Capitalists and large syndicates will, no doubt, in time absorb most of the claims, but in order to do so they will have to purchase each separate mining right or claim from the individual holders in the country. The cost of a mining license is 1s.; the registration and inspection fees amount to about 17s.; and on the payment of these nominal sums any man can prospect on his own account, and, if lucky, possess his portion of the golden reefs; owners of adjacent claims can unite in little syndicates, as they are now doing in many cases, while many an artisan and small farmer will acquire a sufficient sum by the sale of his claims to give him a good start in the new

[1] The right to peg out a much greater number of claims has, in certain instances, been granted to individuals who have rendered special services.

country. The Company exacts no rent on mining claims, but when arrangements are made for the flotation of any mining property into a joint-stock company, the Chartered Company is entitled to one-half of the vendor's scrip. The system practically comes to this: the Chartered Company allows a man to peg out five claims for himself on the condition that, while doing so, he pegs out another five claims for the Company. But, as a matter of fact, each case is treated on its merits, and in every flotation that has come under my notice the Company has agreed to take as its share considerably less than the specified 50 per cent. of the scrip.[1]

In the Transvaal things are very different; the capitalist has it all his own way, the poor man has no chance. There the heavy monthly rent that has to be paid on each claim precludes any but the wealthy from engaging in mining enterprise. On that goldfield, again, it is not

[1] Lord Grey, while addressing a deputation at Fort Salisbury last August, pointed out that the right to 50 per cent. seldom entitled the Chartered Company to more than a quarter interest in the Company floated.

necessary that a man should apply in person for his mining license. A resident in the country is in no better position than one living in a foreign land, for the latter can readily obtain a mining license through the holder of his power of attorney. This system opened an easy road to fraud, of which the Johannesburg speculators were not slow to avail themselves. Should a capitalist need a certain number of licenses he had but to present himself at the mining office, and produce so many powers of attorney drawn up in the names of his wife, his children down to the baby in arms, of Tom, Dick, and Harry in different parts of the world, of men long since dead, and even of people who never had any existence whatever. Corrupt officials connived at the trick; bundles of these sham powers of attorney were hawked about, and a license, taken out in legitimate manner by a man living in the country, had no more value than one of these forged documents. Several other of the Chartered Company's regulations could be adduced as showing an intention to profit by the experiences of neighbouring communities. The rights of the individual immigrant are carefully safeguarded, and Matabeleland will not be permitted to fall into the rings of unscrupulous speculators.

I have already pointed out that considerable depression has recently prevailed among the Mashonaland settlers, who consider that Buluwayo's boom has been at the expense of Mashonaland's prosperity. In every township they have been holding indignation meetings, at which they have aired their various grievances, and in many cases have blamed the Chartered Company for misfortunes which cannot fairly be laid to its charge. Their most serious grievance of all is the alleged tendency of the Chartered Company's mining regulations to prevent the influx of much-needed capital into the country. The Company's claim to 50 per cent. of the vendor's scrip on the flotation of a mining property into a joint-stock company was, I found, the one feature in the mining law which was wholly objectionable in their eyes. It was in vain to remind them that the Chartered Company has invariably made arrangements to accept a smaller share of the scrip (about 33 per cent., for example, in cases I know of). They maintain that such a claim on the part of the Company, on the discovery and flotation of a good property, is a severe tax on capital and a check to enterprise, and that the holding of so large a proportion of the scrip by the Chartered Company gives it the control of the subsidiary mining company, a condition which would make capitalists fight shy of the undertaking. The objection appears to be a frivolous one. The fact that so important and responsible a Corporation as the British South Africa Company —whose interest it is to maintain its high name, to advance the prosperity of its territories, and to obtain a revenue—possesses a considerable stake in the mining companies, must certainly act as a security to the investing public, and prove a protection against bogus flotations. The 50 per cent. clause, far from repelling capital, should have the effect of attracting it. The Company is entitled to its share of the mines, whether it receives it in the form of rent, royalty, or otherwise, and the scheme which has been adopted appears to be the most advantageous for all parties. As the Chartered Company practically takes nothing from the prospector until he has made a rich discovery and can well afford to pay, he has little cause to grumble ; if he is a man of some means there is nothing to prevent him developing his property himself and pocketing all the profits, for the Company can claim nothing unless flotation takes place. There are, I believe, some people in Mashonaland who would scarcely be content were the Chartered Company to make them a present of all its lands and reefs.

Mr. John Hays Hammond, the distinguished American mining expert, who is acknowledged to be the greatest living authority on quartz mines, is now travelling in Matabeleland and Mashonaland. He represents a very large amount of American capital, which he is investing in such mining properties as he approves of. Of the general prospects of these goldfields he has already given a very favourable report. Mr. Hammond is now also mining adviser to the Chartered Company, and in consequence of his

representations to Mr. Rhodes the Company's
mining regulations have been considerably
modified. The new Mining Law was drafted by
Mr. Hammond, and, as a representative of
capital, he finds no fault with the 50 per cent.
clause. Since I wrote the above, which appeared in the form of a newspaper article, I
have met Mr. Hammond and talked the subject
over with him. He has kindly furnished me
with a description of the new Mining Laws and
a statement of his own views, of which the
following is an abstract :—

The new Mining Law which has just been
adopted by the British South Africa Company
has been primarily based upon the American
Mining Law. The resemblance is, however,
rather general than special. In the adaptation
of the American Mining Law various objectionable features have been eliminated, many im-
provements and modifications, dictated both by
American and South African experience, have
been introduced ; administrative provisions of
the Transvaal Law, proved by extended local
experience to present certain practical advan-

Mission hospital, Umtali, 1894 — originally built as a "Palace" for Bishop Knight-Bruce and converted after his departure

Construction work in Gwelo, 1894

Rhodesia's eastern gateway: Chimoio, between Umtali and **Beira**

Street scene in early Beira

tages, have been incorporated, with the result
that the new Law may fairly be said to combine
the merits of two dissimilar systems, and this
without sacrifice or compromise in matters of
principle.

The chief difference between the American
and Transvaal Mining Laws may be briefly
stated as follows :—The Transvaal Law gives to
a claim-holder the right of mining all such portions of a mineral deposit as may lie vertically
below the surface of his claim. The American
confers the same right, and in addition grants
the privilege of following a reef on its 'dips,
spurs, and angles,' even when this involves its
pursuit outside the boundaries of the ground
situated vertically below the surface of a claim.
In other words, the owner of the outcrop, or its
equivalent, is entitled to the whole of the deep
level areas, and thus the distinction between
outcrop and deep level properties, to which in
the Transvaal considerable prominence has been
given, is at once abolished. In the application
of the American principle, however, the Chartered Company's Law is in many important

respects superior to the American, which, having
suffered in the first instance from lack of sufficient definition, has had to be continuously
supplemented by judicial decisions, with the
inevitable result that laborious pruning and
codification would now be necessary were it
desired to give it succinctness and comprehen-
sive exposition. The framers of the Chartered
Company's Law have had the advantage of
commencing where the American Law leaves off.
Codification has been possible, whilst opportunity has at the same time been afforded for
the introduction of amendments in respect of
many matters wherein errors of principle have
insensibly arisen in the United States practice.
Thus, in particular, fixed rules for the determination of the extent of the ' extra-lateral rights '
in individual cases have been laid down, whilst
no condition has been imposed rendering the
enjoyment of these contingent upon the presence
of the ' apex ' of the reef within the boundaries
of a pegged-out claim ; the Chartered Company's
Law in this respect exhibiting a marked improvement upon the American.

As regards the relative sizes of claims in the Transvaal and in the British South Africa Company's territories respectively, it may be stated that in the former a claim measures 150 feet on the line of reef, and 400 feet on the dip, and in the latter 150 feet along the reef, and 600 feet on the dip. Whilst, however, in the Transvaal only one claim may be pegged out under one license, in the Chartered Company's territories a block of ten claims may be located, or an area equal to fifteen times the area of a Transvaal claim, carrying with it the further right of indefinite pursuit of a reef upon its dip, rendering the value of such an area for mining purposes possibly equal to fifty or sixty times that represented by a Transvaal claim. To hold such a block in the Transvaal a prospector would have to pay to the Government monthly a minimum amount of five shillings for each claim of which it was composed, such license moneys constituting an incessant drain upon his resources, and, in the majority of instances, absolutely preventing any comparatively poor man from acquiring mining property. In marked contrast to this, the Chartered Company requires practically no payment for licenses prior to flotation, and only stipulates as a condition of tenure that a far from excessive amount of *bonâ fide* development work shall be annually performed. In other directions also, the interests of the legitimate prospectors have been carefully safeguarded. In the Transvaal the ground open to prospectors generally is exceedingly limited; thus, in the absence of special agreement with the owners of private farms, it is confined to such portions of proclaimed farms as have failed to be considered sufficiently valuable to be taken up by the owners and their friends prior to proclamation. In the Chartered Company's territories private and public grounds are alike open, whilst further protection is afforded by the fact that, prior to the location of any claim, discovery of ' reef in place ' has been made a *sine quâ non*. By this means the locking up of large tracts of unproved ground for purposes of speculation will be prevented, and all alike will enjoy an equal chance of profiting by a first discovery.

Summing up, therefore, it will at once be evident that the interests of a prospector will be far better protected in the Chartered Company's territories than in the Transvaal. In the first place, his operations will not be confined to an artificially restricted area; in the second place, on discovery of a reef he will be permitted to peg out a substantial area of mining ground, which he will hold practically free of expense, the only condition of tenure being the performance of a limited amount of development work, which it will be in his own interests to execute. In the third place, the absence of excessive indirect taxation and the presence of cheap labour will both facilitate mining work and reduce expenses.

Under these circumstances the claim preferred by the Chartered Company to share with the prospector the rewards of his discoveries can at once be justified. The paramount right of the Company to all minerals occurring within its domains is not disputed. This includes the right of selection of any mineral-bearing areas for its own purposes. Its action as regards

prospectors will, when analysed, be found to
amount to nothing more than deferred selection.
In the first instance, it places prospectors in a
position to acquire and hold far larger mining
properties than the same men under the same
conditions would be able to take up and retain
in the Transvaal. That a portion of the ground
thus acquired should be held in trust for the
Company is a reasonable demand. The prospector is placed in precisely the same position
as if the rights conferred by his prospecting
license had in the first instance been somewhat
less generously bestowed. No call is made upon
him until such time as he is in a position to
deal with his property. No hardship is accordingly entailed upon him, and the facts only
require to be stated to afford convincing
demonstration that the outcry which has been
raised in certain quarters against the Company's
action in this matter has been based upon an
utter misconception of the circumstances.

VI

THE CHARTERED COMPANY'S GOLDFIELDS

(a) In Matabeleland

By August last upwards of 51,000 claims
had been pegged out and registered in Matabeleland and Mashonaland, upon which all fees
had been paid. These claims placed side by
side would form a belt of 1,400 miles in length,
a fact which will give some idea of the extent
of the goldfields. Of these, 15,000 claims were
pegged out in Matabeleland within six months
of the occupation, and new reefs are being con-
tinually discovered.

Glowing as are the accounts of rich finds
that reach us from Matabeleland, I doubt
whether they are exaggerated, as a rule ; but
of course up till now a limited amount of development has been done, few shafts have yet

been sunk to any depth, and little, therefore, is known of the real value of the reefs. When I was in the country our hopes were based on little more than the very encouraging promises of the surface scratchings, but of the extent of the auriferous reefs and of the marvellous richness of the surface quartz there could be even then no manner of doubt. The experts I met declared that in no country they know of is there so much visible gold as in Matabeleland—not that this is necessarily a good sign. They brought in specimens from all parts of the country, which not only betrayed their glittering wealth to the eye, but also panned out well. They all appeared to be very satisfied with their discoveries, and agreed that if but one-tenth of the reefs do not belie their present wonderful promise the prosperity of this country is assured. It was extremely improbable, they argued, that the auriferous quartz lay on the surface only; it would be an unprecedented phenomenon were all these reefs to pinch out. It would be as if Nature had planned a cruel practical joke on a gigantic scale, with which to befool the world's gold-seekers. The letters I have recently received from friends in Matabeleland show that the development which is now being energetically carried on throughout the goldfields quite confirms the high expectations that were entertained by old miners from the beginning.

It appears that there are two main gold belts in Matabeleland, one extending from Tati to the Hartley Hill district, in a north-easterly direction, and another extending from Buluwayo eastwards to connect with the Victoria goldfields. The four principal goldfields discovered up till now in Matabeleland are known as the Gwailo, the Bembezi, the Motoppo, and the Mavin. I have visited several of the reefs in these districts and seen pannings taken from a great many claims, with results which I shall describe further on.

So far, very few claims have been pegged out on virgin reefs; the prospectors, as a rule, have merely annexed the ancient workings with which the country is honeycombed. Who those miners of old may have been, Portuguese, Phœnician, or Arabian, is still a mystery, for the natives have preserved no traditions concerning them. The discovery of two old cannons on a ruined fort commanding some disused workings, not far from Buluwayo, seems to show that the Portuguese, if not the first seekers after the precious metal in that region, did at any rate prosecute mining operations of a superficial description some 200 years ago. Most of the workings are undoubtedly of far greater antiquity; but the workers have left few traces behind them to show of what age or race they were. The origin of the wonderful Zimbabwe ruins, the soil round which is full of gold beads, chains, and other ornaments, seems to be still a matter of vague conjecture, and even the interesting discovery of a copper coin of the reign of Antoninus Pius, at the bottom of an ancient shaft near Umtali, does not throw much light on the history of these mines. Whoever the unknown people may have been who worked here, they must have drawn an immense quantity of gold from every part of Mashonaland and Matabeleland. As a rule their workings are superficial, and in many cases they have only removed a portion of the outcrop,

None of their shafts have been sunk below
the average water level, which shows that they
possessed no appliances for pumping. Their
processes must have been of a very crude
description ; it is evident that they could only
make the richest quartz pay, so have left untouched a seemingly unlimited amount of auriferous reef, despised by them as of too poor a
quality, but good enough to prove highly profitable to the modern miner with his improved
methods, and with really hard quartz they could
not deal at all.   On some hill sides, where there
is no water to contend with, our prospectors have
cleared out ancient shafts to a depth of 100 feet
and more. Ancient alluvial workings also
abound all over the country, and in fact, so
thorough has been the exploration in the past,
that though our prospectors have reported alluvial goldfields at the head waters of the Lunde
and elsewhere, no alluvial that would pay white
men to work has yet been discovered.

The American and Australian experts in the
country have expressed themselves very well
satisfied with the appearance of the Matabeleland

G 2

reefs, which are generally found on a formation
of slate, sandstone, and schist. They consider
the country is highly mineralised throughout.
Mr. Hammond has visited all the mining districts of Matabeleland and Mashonaland. He
states that from a geological point of view the
indications are favourable, that the reefs belong
to the class known as fissure veins, which insures
their persistency in depth as well as laterally.
He satisfied himself on this point, the importance
of which can be understood when it is remembered that it was first reported that the ore
bodies belonged to the class known as segregated
veins, which are always very limited in depth.
‘ Of course, only by thorough and extensive
development can the pay-shoots on the reefs be
found and followed up,’ explained Mr. Hammond,
‘ but pay-shoots there are.’   ‘ The quartz veins,’
he reports, ‘ are very similar to those of California, carrying free gold, iron, copper, pyrites,
galena, and zinc blends.’   The transport of
batteries to this remote region will be exceedingly costly for some time to come ; but
notwithstanding this, seeing that fuel and water

are everywhere abundant, and that cheap native labour is procurable, it is estimated that quartz yielding 10 or 12 dwts. to the ton ought to pay very well, even at present.   Capital is now flowing into the country and machinery is being set up, so that it should not be long before deeper workings prove whether this is indeed, what it is believed to be by many, one of the richest goldfields in the world.

A short description of those portions of the gold belt which I visited myself may prove of interest, as giving some idea of the prospects of the country.   I have already spoken of the farming possibilities of the High Veldt in the Gwailo district.   This district has undoubtedly a great future before it, for not only is the best farming land in the country included within its area, but it also contains what promises to be the richest goldfield in Matabeleland.   The site for the Gwailo township has been well chosen.   It is situated under a wooded hill near the source of the Gwailo river, about 110 miles from Buluwayo.   The gold-bearing reefs are from twelve to thirty miles from the township, in a mountainous country where fuel is abun dant. The hills are overgrown with mountain acacia and yellow wood, the latter of which is fit for sawing, and is employed for timbering mines and other purposes. The whole district is very well watered, and there are many perennial streams which will be available for water-power, even through the dry season, if native reports prove accurate. Apparently the only drawbacks to the region—and sportsmen will soon remedy that—are the numerous lions, which often devour the oxen and donkeys of the prospectors.

The marvellous mineral wealth of the district is attracting numbers of white men, and even so far back as last April, when I was there, some 200 prospectors were encamped amid the ancient gold workings with which this portion of the country is honeycombed. I met several of these prospectors, and found all were sanguine and satisfied with their discoveries. At that time some 2,000 claims had already been pegged out by Sir John Willoughby's syndicate, the Mashonaland Development Company, the Bechuanaland Exploration Company, the Buluwayo Syndicate, and the Mashonaland Agency; and development work was being pushed on with all possible speed.   Many prospectors were also pegging out on their own account, and there was room for hundreds more.   Since then the township has sprung up and will soon be a considerable place; further valuable discoveries have been made, and the number of white men has greatly increased.   Stands in the township are fetching very good prices.

In no part of Mashonaland or Matabeleland did the ancients carry out such extensive workings as in this district, and these workings are deeper as a rule than they are elsewhere; it is evident that this was one of their most profitable goldfields.   The Dunraven reef, one of the most promising, on which Sir John Willoughby's syndicate has pegged out forty claims, will serve as an example of what has been discovered here.   This reef is on the usual formation of slate, sandstone, and schist.   The outcrop is traceable on thirty out of the forty claims. The ancients have worked upon the reef throughout its length, but have left it untouched for a breadth of four feet. The quartz is soft and of a dull white colour, having the appearance of loaf sugar, and carrying no visible gold; not the sort of stuff a prospector would as a rule expect much of, but it is likely to prove as rich as any quartz in the country. I saw the panning of some samples from the solid outcrop, which showed a prospect of from ten to fifteen ounces. Fair specimens taken from thirty of the claims showed an average prospect of over two ounces. This reef can be developed at very small cost; for, situated as it is on the slope of the hill, it can be worked by adits alone. Mr. MacIntyre, the manager of the syndicate, assured me that three levels could be opened out without sinking any shaft, and that this would give 300 feet of backs, opening up sufficient ore, at the very lowest estimate, to keep a twenty stamp battery constantly running for four years.

The Bembezi also is a very promising goldfield. Amongst others is what has been named the Queen's reef. The ancient workings on this reef consist of a trench of an average depth of nine or ten feet, extending along the line of reef for 200 yards. The water level is soon reached, so the old miners were unable to work to any depth. This reef is from ten to twelve feet in width. A bar of quartzite, eighteen inches wide, and carrying twelve to fifteen pennyweights, runs along the middle of the reef. The reef is vertical. Shafts have been sunk into it to a considerable depth by the Willoughby syndicate, and the ore that has been brought up looks very good, showing a prospect of more than two ounces. Two miles from the Queen's is the Royal Reef, on which the same syndicate has pegged out ninety claims. This reef, from four to five feet in width, is apparently continuous, without a break in it. Throughout the claims the outcrop appears, and the ancient workings are considerable. Pannings showed a prospect of from two to three ounces.

I visited the Mavin district, and found several prospectors at work amid some very likely-looking reefs under the Khobeli Hill. We found visible gold in all directions among the ancient workings, and pannings taken from the walls of the old shafts showed very good prospects. This district too is attracting numbers of white men at present; and still further to the north, at the head-waters of the Sebakwe, some adventurous prospectors, as far back as February last, discovered reefs of extraordinary richness in a wild and uninhabited country abounding in big game. The claims there pegged out by some fortunate friends of mine have turned out very well indeed. I have selected the above properties for mention because I have some personal knowledge of them. There are many others, no doubt as good, some possibly better; but these will serve as fair examples. The considerable development of Matabeleland properties that has taken place since I was in the country appears to have proved that the surface prospects have not been misleading, and that the reefs are no more likely to 'pinch out' here than on other South African goldfields.

With regard to the presence of other minerals in Matabeleland but little is yet known. Coal has been discovered, and iron is plentiful. At Iron

Mine Hill, between Gwailo and Fort Charter, I
saw the trenches of the extensive workings from
which the natives for generations have extracted
the iron of which they make their assegais.
Large deposits of salt are also found in the pans
to the westward of Buluwayo.

(b) In Mashonaland.

When we turn to Mashonaland it is possible
to speak somewhat more definitely of its prospects as a gold-producing country.   The surface
indications are much the same in both territories ; but in Mashonaland two years' exploration and more has been done, many mines have
been developed, and the auriferous reefs have
been proved to run deep and broad.   And yet,
because so far there has been but a limited
output, many people at home are of opinion that
the Mashonaland goldfields have failed ; and in
some newspapers I still find it boldly asserted
that there is no gold at all in the country.
Many do not seem to realise that a goldfield in
so remote a region cannot be developed in a

few months. As a matter of fact, it is marvellous that so much has already been done under the particularly unfavourable conditions which have prevailed here up till now. Had it not been for the causes to which I have before alluded, viz. the impossibility of obtaining a sufficiency of native labour until the Matabele war had brought security to the frontier, the difficulty and cost of communication, and the lack of capital, a considerable output would ere this have clearly demonstrated that Mashonaland is one of the greatest gold-producing countries in the world. There is no reason to think that this territory, as regards its mining possibilities, is inferior to Matabeleland, for that up till now it has produced so little is no evidence of its worthlessness. At present all goods have to be carried here from the termini of the Cape or Transvaal railway systems on ox waggons along many hundreds of miles of difficult road, at extravagant cost. The freight to Mashonaland *viâ* Natal, the shortest and cheapest route, amounts to 30*l.* a ton, and it is estimated that on the average the expense of transport trebles

the original prices of commodities.   As an example of the tax that is imposed on enterprise
by the existing cost of transport, I may mention
that 10,000*l.* has to be paid for the carriage of
a twenty stamp battery to the Victoria district.
Such charges, of course, check the development
of a country, and the introduction of mining
and other machinery has in many cases been
postponed until communication has been made
easier and cheaper.   This the Beira railway will
shortly do.   It is difficult for one who has not
visited this country to realise how pressing is
the need for the completion of this line.   It will,
as I shall show in another chapter, bring Salisbury within a few days of the coast, and reduce
freights by two-thirds.

By August last nearly 37,000 claims had
been pegged out in Mashonaland—that is, 3,560
in the Salisbury, 6,150 in the Victoria, 10,150
in the Manica, 6,510 in the Mazoe, 2,600 in the
Lo Magundi, and 7,590 in the Umfuli district.
Mashonaland has passed through a long period
of depression, but the tide has already turned.
Numbers of settlers of the right sort are now

entering the country by way of Beira, while capitalists, at last reassured as to the safety of the land—notably American capitalists, who sent their experts out before them to spy out its richness—are embarking in large speculations on the Mashonaland gold reefs, and arrangements are being made for the flotation of several properties. On some of these properties extensive development has been carried out ; five and ten stamp batteries have been erected, and quantities of rich quartz are ' at grass.' When I was in the country, in May, only one battery had started work since the war ; but since then milling has commenced in earnest, and we shall not have to wait much longer for results.

Fort Salisbury itself is the centre of a considerable mining district, and, as this township will always remain the seat of government and capital of both territories, it is sure to be a flourishing place. It is, perhaps, the healthiest of the Mashonaland townships. The beautiful mountainous country of Mazoe has attracted a number of prospectors who have great faith in the future of its extensive goldfields. Of the more distant Lo Magundi district, we shall probably hear a good deal in the near future. Some of the shrewdest miners in South Africa maintain that the richest reefs in all the Chartered Company's territories are those of this gold belt. At this moment prospectors who represent influential syndicates are there exploring and pegging out their claims ; and men who have travelled throughout these regions are of opinion that if a payable alluvial goldfield is to be found anywhere in Rhodesia it will be in Lo Magundi's country.

The best known and most developed goldfields of Mashonaland are those of the Victoria and Manica districts. I travelled through both districts and visited some of the principal mines, a description of which, as I found them at the end of last May, will show to what extent mining operations have already been prosecuted in Mashonaland. I do not mention these particular mines because I have any reason to suppose that they are the best in the country, but because they happen to be the ones I visited.

A two and a half days' journey by coach will

bring the traveller from Fort Salisbury to Victoria, Mashonaland's second township, a far more prettily situated place than the seat of government. It is built on a grassy platform at the meeting of two rivers, the Mshagaske and the Macheke, whose clear waters alternately rush over sands and rocky boulders and repose in deep still pools teeming with crocodiles. From the township, standing as it does at some height above the neighbouring country, a fine view is commanded in every direction over leagues of breezy pasture, dotted with thickets of dark bush, while all round, but not so near as to shut out the health-giving wind, are wooded mountain ranges of bold outline, through whose gaps glimpses are caught of still higher and more distant purple domes, these last containing the golden reefs which are this country's hope. Victoria does not present the ugly, bare appearance of most new colonial settlements. It is a smart, pretty little township of neat red brick houses with verandahs, and gardens of homely English flowers. Even the fort, hurriedly raised at the time of the Matabele scare, is almost picturesque.

The mud houses, of which there are still many,
deep-eaved with thatched roofs, have a comfort-
able old-world air; and when the avenues of
blue gum trees are fully grown this will look
even more charming and cheerful a place than
it does now. For some unexplained reason
there is a good deal of fever here, but this, no
doubt, will gradually disappear. Victoria was
very quiet when I was there; there had been an
exodus of two-thirds of its inhabitants to boom-
ing Matabeleland; most of the houses were shut
up, and there were scarcely more than one hun
dred white men left. This almost deserted village,
like Salisbury, was in a depressed condition.
The settlers that remained were full of their
grievances, and did not stint themselves in the
exercise of their British privilege of grumbling,
but I met none who had lost faith in the
country itself. A number of excellent mining
properties are scattered over the Victoria district, and on several of these sufficient work has
been done to prove that the reefs are deep and
rich, and that their early 'pinching out' need
not be feared.

H

While I was staying at Victoria I visited, among others, the Cotopaxi reef, a property which has perhaps been more fully developed than any in the district ; the American experts are highly pleased with it. Mr. Clark, a high authority, who is working in co-operation with Mr. Hammond, told me that the aspect of the country, the character of the reef, and the intelligent manner in which the work was being carried on, recalled to his mind the first-class Californian mining properties. A pleasant ride across the veldt, now by the side of palmetto-fringed streams, now through coarse grass which rose two feet above a horseman's head, and now through groves of acacia, wild apples, and Kaffir oranges, brought me to the foot of a lofty peak of pyramid shape, with bare granite crags at top, but elsewhere covered with trees, whose foliage was of ruddy, golden, and other rich autumnal tints ; and half-way up a steep shoulder of this peak, at the head of a romantic gully, I saw the white buildings in the vicinity of the mine. It is approached by a well-constructed road, which winds up the gully ; on either side the rocky slopes are overgrown with mountain acacias of large size (which supply the necessary timber for the shafts and drives), beautiful pink-blossomed creepers depending from their branches. From the residential buildings a magnificent view is obtained over the hills and plains ; it would be difficult to find anywhere else a mining property so picturesquely situated. But it is something more than picturesque. The Goldfields of Mashonaland Company has pegged out seventy claims on this reef, and their extensive workings have proved that they here possess an enormous body of auriferous quartz of uniform character and richness. On this highly-favoured property Nature seems to have done all she could to make easy the extraction of the gold from the mountain side : there is an abundance of fuel and water in the im-mediate neighbourhood ; there is no danger of the mine flooding, and pumps are not needed, for, situated as the reef is on a steep hill side, all the working can be done by adits, and the quartz from every part of the mine is brought to the lower of the two existing levels

H 2

and carried to the open down a drive 400 feet
in length. Development will consequently be
very cheap and unattended with difficulty.

I was hospitably received by the staff of
carefully selected Cornishmen who have so
diligently and intelligently carried on the development of this fine property. They are evidently very keen and proud of their mine, as all
true Cornish miners should be: they have
certainly good reason to be proud, for this is a
model mine, and while there has been no extravagant expenditure and no waste of labour,
short-sighted economy has been avoided. Money
has been well laid out to procure the best of
plant, and all work has been thorough. Mr.
Morrish, the manager, has proved himself to be
a master of his profession. There are no daub
huts here; all the buildings are of substantial
brick and iron. The staff is most comfortably
housed. To carry the quartz from the mine, a
solidly laid tramway passes down the lower
drive, and thence for about half a mile down the
gully to the ten stamp battery, one of Sandy-
croft's latest. Only a year since this was a

desolate hill side, inhabited by wild beasts alone ; and it is indeed amazing that so much has been done, despite the compulsory cessation of all work for some time before and during the Matabele war (when all the Mashonas working on the mine took refuge in the mountain tops), and despite the fever, which is exceptionally severe here and has prostrated the majority of the white men. The mine is in a highly advanced state, and a large amount of development has already been accomplished: 2,000 feet of the reef have been opened out, and a great quantity of quartz is at grass. In default of some necessary piping, which was still on the road, the battery was idle when I visited the mine ; but it has since then set to work, and there will be plenty for it to do for years to come. I explored the shafts and drives, and saw the visible gold on many portions of the walls. I witnessed some remarkable panning not only from the quartz at grass, but from samples taken fairly from different parts of the mine. In one case several handfuls of the finer stuff were taken haphazard from the stacked quartz. This was panned as it was, without being crushed, and showed an extraordinary tail of coarse gold that ran right round the dish.   There were a number of plump Mashonas, Matabele, and Shangans at work on the mine, and the manager told me that since the war he had not experienced the slightest difficulty in obtaining as much native labour as he required.

A two and a half days' journey by coach through a delightful country brings the traveller from Fort Salisbury to Umtali, the capital of the Manica district, undoubtedly far the most prettily situated of Mashonaland's townships. From the sloping ground on which stand the police camp and the hospital, one looks down upon the little settlement half a mile away, its red brick houses scattered over a green flat, bold, wooded hills surrounding it on every side, while in the background towers above the lesser heights the rugged mountain, purple in the distance, on which is the stronghold of the troublesome chieftain Umtassa, the self-styled king of the Manicas.   Umtali, like Salisbury and Victoria, has its grievances, holds indignation meetings, and sends querulous telegrams to Cape Town; but the people, realising that the long wanted Beira railway is being vigorously pushed forward at last, and that the day of prosperity is nigh, are beginning to shake off their depression. Umtali has indeed good reason to be hopeful. It is most favourably situated; all the rich reefs in the Manica district are in its close vicinity; the very hills which overshadow the township are full of workings, ancient and modern, while the most promising properties— the Rezende, the Penhalanga, and the Maggie, for example—are within a few miles of it. Consequently, when the Beira railway has been extended to Umtali the mines will be working under far more advantageous and economical conditions than any others within the Chartered Company's territory; ore of much lower grade will be found to be payable here than could possibly prove so in the remoter districts of Mashonaland and Matabeleland, and there is no reason why most commodities should not then be as cheap in Umtali as in Cape Town; for, as the Chartered Company imposes no custom

duties, the 3 per cent. transit duty, which
Portugal is entitled by the Convention to levy
on all goods passing through her territory into
Mashonaland, will be the only tax to which they
will be subjected.

I have already spoken of the magnificent
agricultural and grazing possibilities of the
beautiful mountainous country between Umtali
and the Portuguese frontier.   The gold belt
extends along these ranges from west to east
for about ten miles in our territory before passing into the debatable land, whose ownership is
still undefined.   On this gold belt, as elsewhere
throughout the country, all enterprise was interrupted for many months by the Matabele war ;
but now the mines are being vigorously developed, and the wealth of the district will, no
doubt, be soon proven to the world by a considerable output of gold.   The people here, all
of whom are in one way or another interested
in the mining industry, are sanguine of their
prospects, and it is evident that the ancients
also thought very highly of this gold belt, for all
the valley bottoms have been turned up with

their alluvial diggings, while the hill sides are full of their rough reef workings.

I visited some of the principal mining properties; among others the Rezende Reef, on which the United Goldfields of Manica Company has pegged out fifty claims (Portuguese claims, each of 100 mètres square). The reef is on the steep slope of a pretty valley, seven miles from Umtali. As we crossed the valley I noticed that the ground was everywhere burrowed with large holes, where the ancients had their alluvial diggings. I was shown the three long adits by which it was hoped that the reef would be cut, and after scrambling for some distance higher up the mountain we came to the outcrop on which the ancients had carried on extensive workings. Experts think highly of this property; the mine can be easily worked; so far as it has been exposed the ore is not refractory, and it assays and pans well. Since I was there the adit has cut into the reef, which is five feet broad and rich.

I also visited the Penhalanga Reef, where the Penhalanga Gold Mining Company has pegged

out fifty claims. The prospects of this property
are considered to be very good. The quartz is
of almost unique character, highly mineralised
and studded with crystals of red chromate of
lead. On entering the main adit by candle-
light, I found that in places it presented a most
curious and beautiful appearance, the walls
glowing and flashing with the blood-red crystals,
as if this were one of those magical jewel-hung
caverns one reads of in the oriental fairy tales.

The debatable land beyond the Crow's Nest
is said to be the part of the country richest in
gold, so it is to be hoped that the arbitration
now proceeding will confirm the Chartered Company's title.

VII

COMMUNICATION

THE difficulty of transport has so far been Mashonaland's great trouble. The distance of the terminus of the Cape railway system at Vryburg to Salisbury is nine hundred miles; the waggon road is of the roughest description; goods, even in the dry season, are often delayed many months on the journey; and during the rainy season, when the rivers are flooded and deep quagmires are formed in the valley bottoms, communication is practically cut off. The road which connects Mashonaland with the Transvaal railway system is somewhat shorter. The Beira route is obviously the natural one into Mashonaland. From that seaport to Umtali is only two hundred and thirty-five miles, and Salisbury is but one hundred and fifty miles further. The road, too, is in good condition. But unfortu-

nately, between the Manica Highlands and the
coast extends a broad belt of swampy lowland,
densely overgrown with tropical bush and forest,
infested by that curse of Africa, the tsetse fly,
whose bite is fatal to horses and cattle. It is
true that goods can be carried through the ' fly '
on ox waggons, and this has often been done ;
but the transport charges are of course almost
prohibitive, based as they are on the certainty
of losing every ox after a few journeys across
this deadly region. Accordingly, up till now,
traders have chiefly relied on the uncertain,
slow, and very costly system of native carriers
for the transport of their goods from the coast.
It was therefore of urgent importance that the
Beira railway should be pushed on as rapidly as
possible, until it had spanned the fly belt, at
least ; and that this work, on which the prosperity of the country so much depends, has
progressed very tardily until quite recently is
due partly to the lack of capital, which came
in by driblets, partly to the fever which proved
very deadly to the white men engaged on the
line, partly to the destructive floods in the rainy

season, and partly no doubt to mismanagement
at the early stages of the undertaking.

What they term the Beira railway fiasco
constitutes the principal grievance of the Mashonaland settlers. The delay in carrying that
railway across the fly has retarded the progress
of the country and maintained the cost of transport from the coast at 30*l*. a ton, so that the
prices of even the necessaries of life are still
extraordinarily high. For the last three years
the settlers have struggled on as best they could,
knowing that the development of the country's
resources would in time bring prosperity within
their reach; but, being for the most part men of
small means, they have found it difficult indeed
to make both ends meet; many have drifted
into debt, and despair of holding out much longer, while not a few have left the country in
disgust. The storekeepers and traders, exacting
the high prices which have crushed the unfortunate settlers, point to the difficulties of
communication and to the transport rates as
their justification, and are ever the most loudly
indignant orators at the public meetings when

the Beira railway is the subject of discussion.
They abuse the whole Beira route in unmeasured
terms ; they condemn the railway as being hope-
lessly ill-constructed, and assert that it is so
carelessly managed that their goods are often
detained for many months at Beira, while they
also suffer heavy losses from theft, their cases
of stores being frequently broken open and
looted in transit. They describe the cart road
between Umtali and the present railway terminus as being in a vile condition, and declare
that the fly belt extends for many leagues
westward of Chimoio, and that until the railway
has been carried to within sixty miles of Umtali
(which cannot be done before the coming rains),
transport riders must expect to lose their oxen
when bringing up goods from the railway to
Mashonaland. The storekeepers have put their
case strongly, but there is another side to this
question. The above statements have been
spread and accepted as true throughout South
Africa and at home, with the result that travellers have been deterred from entering Mashonaland by the natural route—the only route that

any one who has tried the others would adopt—
and that merchants are still forwarding their
goods *viâ* Vryburg and Pretoria.

I travelled last June from Umtali to Beira,
and have come to the conclusion that, though
the Mashonalanders had an undoubted grievance,
their spokesmen have grossly exaggerated the
facts, and by doing so have considerably preju-
diced the interests of the country. It is not
difficult to understand the motives of those who
have disseminated these misstatements. After
making every allowance for the cost of transport
and other considerations, I maintain that the
middlemen in Rhodesia have from the commencement combined to keep up an unwarrant-
ably high standard of prices, which exceeds
anything that I have experienced in other parts
of the world more remote and difficult of access
than this. The average storekeeper in Mashonaland expects to make his fortune within the
course of a year or two, at the expense of his
fellows—chiefly, of course, by the sale of vile
whisky. Were this a rich alluvial goldfield,
or were there some other exceptional circum-

stances which enabled the settlers to acquire
wealth rapidly, storekeepers would be justified
in grasping their share of the abnormal prosperity by making abnormal charges : but such
charges are preposterous in Mashonaland in its
present state of depression; for, as things are
now, the non-producing middlemen who grumble
the loudest are the only members of the community who are enriching themselves.

It must be difficult for youngsters in the
Civil Service, and others of limited income, to
make both ends meet in these townships,
wherein I have seen articles, the cost of transport of which was trifling in proportion to their
value, sold at as much as six times their retail
price in Cape Town. The Chartered Company
has endeavoured, as I have pointed out, to
make of this a good poor man's country, but
this intention is frustrated by the middlemen.
The poor man is crushed by the expense of
living in the towns; if he can afford to import
his stores from down-country, to buy his stand
and build his own house, he can live economic-
ally; but otherwise it is difficult for him to do

A Matabele kraal

A defensive kraal, Mashonaland

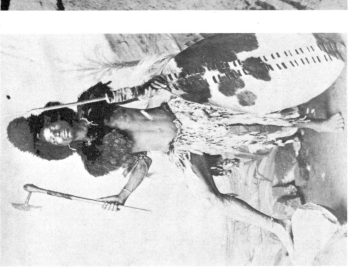

Matabele warrior

Matabele women, Matopo Hills

so. Four pounds a month is charged for one little room in Salisbury, and I found that the rent of a small house, which cost 800*l.* to build, amounted to 360*l.* a year. I may mention, as an example of the profits that are being made, that when I was in Buluwayo a bottle of whisky cost five times as much there as it did in the Bechuanland Border Police canteen forty miles further on. The firm that supplied the police made a very good profit out of the transaction, so what must have been the profit of the Buluwayo trader? Some well-meaning people may urge that in this particular instance a high price is an advantage to the community, and perhaps it would be so were it not that prices can be ruinous without being prohibitive in the least. Those who drink immoderately will drink the same amount whatever be the cost, and with many men the high prices, leading to hopeless debt and so to recklessness, but drive to heavier drinking than would be the case were stimulants cheaper.

The smaller shopkeepers often explain that the matter does not rest with them, for, living

I

from hand to mouth, having no capital and little credit, they cannot buy in a cheap market, but have perforce to purchase their goods from other up-country traders at extravagant prices, and, when given credit, must pay interest at usurious rates. In some cases the goods have passed through the hands of half a dozen middlemen, each of whom has taken his profit, before the retail shopkeeper, having first added his own profit, sells them to the consumer with all their accumulation of exorbitant profits piled upon the original price. But the large trading societies in this country have no such excuse as this. They have capital behind them, can buy in the cheapest market, and are therefore far more to blame than the smaller fry. Each year these traders neglect to import a sufficiency of stores during the dry season when the roads are open; it pays them best not to do so, for the consequent scarcity of commodities during the rainy season affords an admirable pretext for pushing prices still further to famine rates. It is the consumer alone who suffers. I believe that the storekeepers, who are the leaders of the present agitation, in their hearts dread the advent of the railway for which they are clamouring ; for not only will it reduce freights by two-thirds, but it will introduce capital and competition, fair profits and fair prices, a state of things which will deprive most of the present grasping and unbusiness-like traders of their occupation. They wish to maintain the existing unsatisfactory system as long as possible ; and it is their policy, while posing as agitators for the public good, to hoodwink the outer world with their unscrupulous misstatements, and prevent a proper appreciation of the great advantages of the Beira route.

These storekeepers, who have not altogether unnaturally taken advantage of their opportunities, will now have to content themselves with reasonable profits, or make room for others. There are clear signs to show that the prosperity of Mashonaland is about to advance by rapid strides, the old rings and monopolies will vanish before competition, and the capital needful to carry on this competition is already on its way here. While at Salisbury I met

some shrewd gentlemen from home who represent some north country capitalists ; they are, I
understand, about to buy stands in the townships, where they will establish large stores.
Their goods will be imported through Beira, and
they are of opinion that they will reap a very
handsome profit indeed if they sell at half the
existing prices.   This enterprise deserves success, and if it abolishes the present system, by
which the middleman grasps everything and
impoverishes his fellow settlers, who have such
difficulty in holding their own in these hard
times, a great boon will have been conferred
upon the country.

I travelled last June from Umtali to Beira,
and I will now describe the route as I found it.
In the first place, the rainy season lasts for only
three months on the east coast, so that the
road should be quite open for at least eight
months of the year, which is ample for all
Mashonaland's needs.   I found that at the time
I made it, the journey of 235 miles from Umtali
to Beira was thus divided—115 by cart road
from Umtali to the terminus of the railway at

75-mile peg; 75 miles by railway to Fontesvilla
on the Pungwe river; and 45 miles by river
steamer from Fontesvilla to Beira. As no
coach was then running, and no waggons were
going down the road, my three companions and
myself had to tramp it to 75-mile peg. At that
season the climate is delicious, bracing, and
healthy. Even were there no railway, this
route to Salisbury would be the pleasantest as
well as the shortest. The cart road has been
put in excellent condition, it is well drained, the
bridges that span the stream are of solid construction, and are capable of resisting the
summer floods. No fault can be found with it:
it is, indeed, the only road worthy of the name
that I have seen in the country, and yet its
supposed bad condition is one of the favourite
themes of the Salisbury orators. I soon began
to realise how reckless had been their mis-
representations. We found a fair hotel every
fifteen miles, and were constantly crossing
streams of clear, cold water. We had to rough it
no more than if we had been taking a walking
tour on the high roads of Normandy. Our

baggage was carried by native bearers, each
man receiving his ten shillings for taking his
50 lbs. load to 75-mile peg. Passing through the
lovely Manica country, with its rolling wooded
hills and fair valleys, we gradually descended
some 4,000 feet to the lowlands. It was perfect
weather for walking, not too hot by day, a fresh
breeze always blowing, while at night and in
the early morning it was almost too cold. A
few marches brought us to the low country,
where the palms, bamboos, and dense undergrowth enabled us to realise that we were
within the tropics, and our path often lay for
miles through rank grass twelve feet and more
in height. We met several trains of coolies
bound for Umtali from the railway terminus,
laden for the most part with cases of beer and
whisky. I may mention that even under the
present expensive system of carriage the freight
of a bottle of whisky to Umtali from Beira
amounts to about one shilling, scarcely enough
to justify the remarkable difference between
Beira and Umtali prices. Even in the heart of
the last rainy season, when the railway com-

munication was interrupted, it was not by any means so impossible to get up goods from below as was alleged by the traders who grabbed their famine profits at that time. I know that for one firm at least whisky was carried across the flooded land all the way from Fontesvilla to Umtali, by bearers, at 1*l.* the case.

On reaching Chimoio, a miserable Portuguese settlement seventy-four miles from Umtali, we satisfied ourselves, after many inquiries, that the report circulated by the Salisbury traders, to the effect that there is tsetse fly in this neighbourhood, was a pure fabrication. The tsetse is never seen at Chimoio, and the western limit of the fly belt is some twenty miles to the eastward of this. It is therefore certain that the railway, when it has been extended to Chimoio, will have completely bridged this belt, and that transport riders need have no fear of taking their waggons to this point. Chimoio will not for long remain the terminus of the railway, for it is a most unhealthy place in the wet season, being surrounded by swamps and wastes of very high grass. Lions abound in the neigh-

bourhood, and are a great nuisance to the
inhabitants.

We came to the formation of the railway at
89-mile peg. Mr. Lawley had then upwards of
2,500 natives at work on the extension, and
labour was obtained without difficulty. Slow as
has been the progress of this railway hitherto,
the necessity of its speedy completion has now
been fully realised; the work is being pushed on
as rapidly as possible, and Mr. Lawley assured
me that, unless some unforeseen accident hap-
pened, the railway would have bridged the fly
and reached Chimoio by the end of October.
This should bring Umtali within four days of
the coast by rail and coach, and the journey
from Beira to Salisbury should not occupy more
than six days.

At 75-mile peg we found that quite a considerable settlement—chiefly of bamboo huts
—had grown up around the terminus. Here
we saw sheds full of stores of all descriptions,
and huge stacks of goods standing by the line,
all awaiting waggons to transport them to
Mashonaland. Some of these goods have been

lying here uncalled for since December, and I
was told that there was another great accumulation of stores at Chimoio, which had been carried
across the fly by native bearers. It was not,
therefore, the fault of the railway company that
there was, even at that late season, a dearth of
necessaries in Mashonaland, and that almost
famine prices prevailed; the traders who
neglected to send down waggons were alone to
blame. We passed no waggons on our way.
If the agitating traders were so anxious to get
their goods up, why had they not long before
had their waggons in readiness at the railway
terminus? Instead of doing this, by dissemina-
ting false reports as to the condition of the road
and rail, they had succeeded in frightening the
transport riders away from this route. The
Trans-Continental Telegraph Company is now
sending its material through the fly belt—which
narrows considerably in the winter months—by
a service of light waggons. Travelling rapidly
backwards and forwards across the infested belt
by night, when the danger is not so great, the
oxen are enabled to make several journeys

before they fall victims to the tsetse. There is
no reason why the traders should not have
organised a similar scheme. Lord Grey, writing
to the 'Times' from Delagoa Bay on Septem-
ber 13, states that even at that date there was an
accumulation of over 1,200 tons waiting at 75-
mile peg for transport waggons to be moved up-
country.

The railway journey to Fontesvilla now
occupies about twelve hours. Having heard
the line so violently abused, we were astonished
to find it in such excellent order. It is, of
course, true that the enterprise was muddled at
first. It is stated on good authority that the line
was not well surveyed ; the rails might with
advantage have been heavier (though I am
assured by those who should know best that
they are strong enough to carry the heaviest
machinery that will be required in Mashonaland), and the earthworks in places should have
been higher. But there is no doubt that the
railway will answer its purpose, and is anything
but the useless concern it is often represented to
be ; it is settling and getting firmer daily, and in

the opinion of experts it will suffer but slight damage in future rainy seasons. A train now runs regularly each way daily, capable of carrying one hundred tons, which is far more than the supply of ox waggons in Mashonaland can possibly cope with.

The railway journey was a pleasant one, sometimes through tropical forest with great trees and dense undergrowth, sometimes across undulating wastes of long grass and bush studded with palms, a great game country where lions and buffalos abound. We saw our first tsetse fly at 45-mile peg, and then, for a few hours, our carriage was crowded with the little pests. We reached Fontesvilla by dinner time, and put up at a very fair hotel, the loud croaking of legions of frogs giving us due notice that we were surrounded by malarious swamps. On the following morning a small steamer took us down the Pungwe river to Beira. The lake-like expanses of the river reaches are bordered by mangroves and dense bush ; the hippopotami are numerous here, and we frequently saw their heads rising above the muddy water.

The tales of the Mashonaland traders, to the effect that their goods are detained at Beira and lost and stolen in transit, have persuaded numbers of merchants that it is unsafe to forward anything by this route. There is absolutely no foundation for these reports. Goods are pushed up from Beira far more rapidly than the consignees can carry them away, and there is no detention of any merchandise save for very good cause, such as the inability of the consignees to pay custom dues and freight. One of the traders, who at a recent meeting complained bitterly of such detention, omitted to explain that he was unable or unwilling to pay the railway charges, and had asked the Company to give him credit. The Company, having had some experience of Mashonaland traders as debtors, refused to open a ledger account with this gentleman, but is quite prepared to despatch his goods to him with all promptitude as soon as he sends payment for their carriage. I have also ascertained that there has been but one instance of loss of goods in transit, when a Kaffir stole some stores of

trifling value ; he was caught, and the owner
was compensated. Such an incident might
have occurred on any line. In short, so far as
the condition of both cart road and railway are
concerned, there appears to be absolutely no
justification for the present agitation in Mashonaland, and I also found that the steamer and
lighter service between Fontesvilla and Beira is
being conducted in a regular and in every way
satisfactory manner. But were the railway to
carry their goods for nothing, and the Chartered
Company to supply them with free waggons at
75-mile peg, I believe that some of these agitators would still find something to growl at.

When I was in the country the rates, inclu-
sive of loading and unloading charges, from
Beira to Umtali, amounted to about 25*l.* a ton,
that is, by lighter to Fontesvilla 1*l.* a ton; by
rail to 75-mile peg, 3*l.* 15*s.* a ton ; and by
waggon from 75-mile peg to Umtali about
1*l.* a hundredweight. Making all allowance
for the ravages of the tsetse fly, this last
charge of 20*l.* per ton for waggon transport
along one hundred and fifteen miles of excellent

road is a preposterous one, the rate being kept up by lack of competition and the widely circulated misstatements as to the various perils of the road. As soon as the railway reaches Chimoio there is no reason why the waggon rates for the remaining seventy-four miles to Umtali should exceed 4s. a hundredweight, or to Salisbury 12s. The waggon rates between Vryburg and Buluwayo—six hundred miles of most difficult road—amount to only 23s. a hundredweight.[1]

We found the much abused Beira to be a clean little place, with good streets and fair stores and hotels. Built as it is on the sandy shore and almost perpetually swept by a fresh wind from the sea, it is undoubtedly healthy, though the neighbouring swampy country is very malarious in the wet season. All the white men on the railway construction were recently down with fever, and a large proportion died. The agitators who so mercilessly abuse those to whom this undertaking was entrusted should call this fact to mind. On one occasion Mr.

---

[1] The railway has reached Chimoio since I wrote the above.

Lawley, in a letter to his directors, explained that his delay in supplying certain reports was unavoidable, as he had lost three bookkeepers in succession of fever in one month, and was without one at the time. However, there is practically no risk for one travelling through the country in the dry season. The Portuguese are waking up to the fact that Beira, being the gateway of the Chartered Company's territory, is likely to become a port of considerable importance, and they now propose, should the capital be forthcoming, to construct a railway from Beira to Fontesvilla. They also have a scheme—a visionary one, I think, and beyond their capacity —to carry another line from Beira to Sena, on the Zambesi, in order to tap the trade of the Zambesi valley, that river gradually becoming unnavigable in consequence of the silting up of its Chinde mouth.

As regards the immediate destination of the railways which are opening up communication between the Chartered Company's territory and the seaports, the Beira railway will shortly be extended to Umtali, while the Northern railway from Cape Town is rapidly being pushed forward in the direction of Buluwayo. Since I was in the country this line has been extended from Vryburg to Mafeking, bringing Matabeleland one hundred miles nearer to civilisation. The line is now to be carried on to Gaberones, and thence to Khama's capital, Palapye. Mr. Rhodes anticipates making an arrangement with the Imperial Government for its extension to Buluwayo itself.

At present the steamer service to Beira amply suffices for the traffic. The Union and Castle lines afford direct communication between Europe and Beira. The Union Company, whose connection with South Africa is of many years' longer standing than that of any other line, and whose vessels have carried on the Cape of Good Hope Mail service under contract with Her Majesty's Government since 1857, has also a contract with the Portuguese Government, under which its finest steamers leave Hamburg and other Continental ports every twenty-eight days, load at Southampton, proceed to Lisbon, Teneriffe and Cape Town, and thence to Delagoa Bay, Beira, Chinde, Mozambique, Ibo and Zanzibar (and intermediate ports), calling at the same places on the homeward journey. So soon as the traffic to Beira increases sufficiently, the Directors of the Company will take steps to meet it.

Pending the completion of these railways, which will prove such an inestimable boon to Rhodesia, the waggon routes are maintained in as good condition as is possible. At the commencement of the winter large gangs of natives, under efficient engineers, repair the damages which the summer floods have inflicted on the roads leading from Mashonaland to the south. The roads from Salisbury to Pretoria, and to the Beira railway through Umtali, are exceptionally good, and a considerable sum is spent on their maintenance. A new road has been opened out between Buluwayo and Salisbury, through Gwailo and Fort Charter. The worst road of all is that between Mafeking and Buluwayo, and the foolish policy which the Imperial Government has pursued with regard to the semi-independent Kaffir chieftains within the Protectorate is to blame for this. It would surely not have

K

been a great hardship on these brawny blacks
who, secure under our protection, acquire wealth
and fatten in lazy peace, were each tribe compelled to keep in repair that section of the high
road which lies within its territory; but instead
of this the Kaffirs are permitted to place ob-
stacles in our way. The very roughest part of
the northern road is that which passes through
Khama's country. The first stage beyond his
capital, for example, is responsible for the death
of many oxen and horses, the road here being
strewn with great boulders and sharp rocks for
many miles. A very little labour on the part of
his people would set this right. But Khama,
whom I believe to be a thoroughly well-
meaning and good man, will not have the road
improved on any account, and I am sorry to
say that the missionaries encourage this teetotal
despot, whom they pet and flatter in an egre-
gious manner, to pursue this policy, which they
maintain is in the interests of Christianity.

This childish attempt at obstruction can of
course do nothing to stay the white man's
advance on the rich territories to the north, and

its only result is the infliction of unnecessary torture on a great number of unfortunate animals.

The coach services throughout Rhodesia have recently been much improved. Coaches run to Buluwayo from both Pretoria and Mafeking. Salisbury is connected with Victoria, Umtali, and the Beira railway by other coach services. The conquest of Matabeleland has opened a shorter route to Fort Salisbury from the south, and for the future the mails, instead of passing through the Transvaal, will be carried across British territory *viâ* Mafeking, Buluwayo, and Fort Charter.

The telegraph system is being spread through this portion of South Africa with extraordinary rapidity. The wire connecting Fort Salisbury with Cape Town has been working for some time. A few months after the termination of the Matabele war the telegraph was carried on from Mafeking through Tati to Buluwayo, and no sooner was this effected than receipts at the rate of 3,000*l.* a year were taken at the Buluwayo telegraph office alone. A line will also be constructed as soon as possible from Fort Salisbury to Umtali and thence to Chimoio, to connect with a telegraph from Beira. The Trans-Continental Telegraph is also progressing apace : the Salisbury-Tete and the Blantyre-Tete sections have been already completed.

TIME OCCUPIED AND FARES ON THE PRINCIPAL ROUTES FROM THE COAST TO MATABELELAND AND MASHONALAND.

I

From Cape Town, viâ Bechuanaland.

Cape Town to Vyrburg by train daily. 44½ hours.

					£	s.	d.
First Class	.	.	.	.	8	11	4
Second ,,	.	.	.	.	5	17	8
Third ,,	.	.	.	.	3	4	6

Vyrburg to Buluwayo by weekly post-cart. Nine days. Fare 29*l.*

Now that the railway has been extended to Mafeking, the journey by this route is cheaper and occupies less time.

II

From Cape Town, viâ the Transvaal.

Cape Town to Pretoria by rail. 58 hours.

					£	s.	d.
First Class	.	.	.	.	11	18	9
Second ,,	.	.	.	.	8	5	6
Third ,,	.	.	.	.	4	13	9

Pretoria to Buluwayo by weekly post-cart. Six days. Fare 22*l.*

Coach from Buluwayo to Salisbury. Five days. Fare 12*l,*

III

From Beira.

From Beira to Fontesvilla by steamer.   One day.   Fare 25s.
From Fontesvilla to Chimoio by train.   One day.   Fare 3l. [?]
From Chimoio to Salisbury by coach.   About four days.
Fare 9l.

Only 25 lbs. of baggage are allowed free on post-carts and
coaches, and for anything beyond that amount prohibitive rates
must be paid.   Heavy baggage must therefore be sent on by
ox-waggon.   The transport riders are generally ready to take
passengers on their waggons.   The rate of progress is very slow,
but the charges are moderate, and one can carry any reasonable
amount of baggage free.   I only had to pay 5l. for my fare from
Mafeking to Buluwayo, with nearly 200 lbs. of baggage.   The
lowest sum (exclusive of cost of provisions on the journey up-
country) for which an emigrant can reach Buluwayo from
England is about 18l.—*i.e.* from Southampton to Cape Town by
Union Steamship, 10l.; railway fare from Cape Town to Pretoria, 4l. 13s. 9d.; by waggon from Pretoria to Buluwayo, about
3l.

VIII

ADMINISTRATION

THE scheme which has now been adopted for the administration of Matabeleland, though criticised as faulty in some of its details, has met with a general approval in South Africa. It was at first feared, and not without reason, that a Crown Colony would be established here; but Her Majesty's Government, bearing in mind that Matabeleland as well as Mashonaland is included within the region described in the Charter as the principal field of the operations of the British South Africa Company, that the concessions held by the Company are applicable to the whole of Lobengula's territory, and that the recent war had been principally carried on at the expense of the Company, decided that it would be right to place Matabeleland under the direct administration of the Company, and that the Company's machinery for government which was at work in Mashonaland should be extended with certain modifications to the newly acquired country. The Company was to be left to govern the entire territory ; but in order that the rights of the natives might be safeguarded, the Imperial Government was to be vested with a somewhat fuller control over the Company than heretofore.

The day will no doubt come when a representative form of government will prevail in Rhodesia. An agitation for an extension of local self-government in the townships has already commenced, and the settlers have also petitioned that one member of the Administrative Council, recently created by the Imperial Government, should be elected by ballot by the residents of the country. To accede to this desire, which is by no means general, but is rather the whim of certain busybodies, is out of the question at this early stage of the country's development, and to hold a general election by ballot would be extremely difficult. This small population, still unsettled, scattered over an immense territory, cannot yet be entrusted with

the control of the affairs of the commonwealth ;
and to invest the communities of the townships
with unlimited borrowing powers would be a
very dangerous experiment. A representative
government, as things are now, would be
prejudicial to the settlers themselves, as the
wisest among them clearly perceive. All acknowledge that capital is the essential need of
Mashonaland and Matabeleland ; the capitalists
who, having confidence in the strong, just and
responsible government of the Company, are
now prepared to invest in this country, develop
its resources, and bring prosperity to all, would
hesitate to do so were their interests to be placed
at the mercy of the irresponsible vote of the
present population. The bankruptcy of townships and a general sense of insecurity would be
the probable result of such a scheme, while the
Chartered Company itself would be prevented
from reaping the fair reward of its exertions, and
of the vast expenditure it has incurred.

Up till now, the Chartered Company's territory has been administered under a one man
government, a benevolent despotism, the best

possible under all the circumstances, the most economical, the most efficient, the most prompt in emergency ; for the Company has had the good fortune of securing the services of the right man, Dr. Jameson, whose energy, whose tact, whose large grasp of every problem and difficult situation, whose high genius for administration can only be fully realised by those who have been in the country and observed him when engaged in the performance of his duties. With his charm of manner, his straightforwardness, and the sound common sense of his arguments, he exerts a great influence over all who come in contact with him ; and on several occasions I have seen a settler who has approached him boiling over with some imaginary grievance rapidly brought to reason by the Administrator, to depart in good humour and quite contented, though not a jot had been conceded to his importunity. In his capacity as Administrator, Dr. Jameson has to refuse many favours, and during the depression which has for some time prevailed in Mashonaland he has had to deal with a great deal of discontent on the part of the

settlers; but, dissatisfied as many of them profess themselves to be with the Company's policy,
the Company's greatest enemy of them all has
nought but words of highest praise and respect
for Dr. Jameson. He is universally popular,
despite the extreme delicacy of his duties and
the firmness with which he supports the Company's interests against its foes.

But a one man government is open to the
serious objection that it is only by occasional
good luck that the right ' one man ' is found ;
and he must be an exceptionally strong man
who would administer Mashonaland. There is a
natural distrust of the one man rule, for, admirable as it may be, it can only be a temporary
expedient. Accordingly, it has been decided to
create in Rhodesia a form of government which
appears to have been modelled on that of the
Indian Viceroy and his Council. The Agreement
entered into between Her Majesty's Government
and the British South Africa Company, executed
on May 23, 1894,[1] provides that the administra-

---

[1] See *Papers Relating to the Administration of Matabeleland and Mashonaland.* Presented to both Houses of
Parliament May 1894. Eyre & Spottiswoode. 1894. [C.—7383.]

tion of the government of the territories bounded by British Bechuanaland, the Bechuanaland Protectorate, the German Protectorate, the rivers Chobe and Zambesi, the Portuguese Possessions and the South African Republic, be conducted by the Chartered Company under an Administrator and a Council of four members, composed of a Judge and three other members, any two members of which shall form a quorum.

That the Imperial Government has reserved to itself a full control of the administration of the Chartered Company's territory will be seen from the following provisions in the Agreement, which ought to satisfy those at home who are jealous or mistrustful of the Company, and who consider it might abuse its power unless efficient safeguards were provided :—

The Administrator shall be appointed by the Company, with the approval of the Secretary of State, and may be removed either by the Secretary of State or by the Company, with the approval of the Secretary of State. He shall, unless sooner removed, hold his office for a term of three years, and after the end of that term shall continue to hold his office until his successor is appointed. An Administrator whose term of office has expired may be reappointed.

The Judge shall be appointed by the Company, with the approval of the Secretary of State, and may be removed only by the Secretary of State. He shall be a member of the Council ex-officio.

The members of the Council, other than the Judge, shall be appointed by the Company, with the approval of the Secretary of State, and may be removed by the Company. On the expiration of two years from the first appointment of members, and on the expiration of every succeeding period of two years, one member of the Council shall retire from office.

When the Administrator or the Judge or other member of the Council resigns, is removed, or dies, the Company shall, within nine months of his resignation, removal, or death, appoint a successor, of whom the Secretary of State approves, and if they fail to do so the appointment may be made by the Secretary of State.

The Administrator shall, as representative of the Company, administer the Government of the said territories, but shall take the advice of his Council in all questions of importance affecting the government of the said territories. If in cases of emergency it shall be impracticable to assemble a quorum, the Administrator may take action alone, but he shall report such action to the Council at its next meeting. If the Administrator dissents from the opinion of the Council, he may overrule their opinion ; but in such case he shall report the matter forthwith to the Company, with the reasons for his action. The Company may rescind the decision of the Administrator.

It shall be lawful for the Administrator, with the concurrence of at least two members of the Council, and with the approval of the High Commissioner, to frame and issue regulations ; and every such regulation, after it has received the approval of the High Commissioner, shall on its promulgation have the force of law. Provided that either the Secretary of State or the Company may veto any such regulation at any time within twelve months of the date of approval by the High Commissioner. In case of the exercise of such veto, the regulation shall be of no force and effect, save as to any act done, right acquired, or liability incurred thereunder before the exercise of the said veto had been communicated to the Administrator and public notice of the same had been given by him.

The Judge shall have jurisdiction over all causes, both civil and criminal, and shall hold courts at such places as may be from time to time prescribed by proclamation of the High Commissioner or by ordinance of the Company. The procedure, rules, and regulations of these courts shall be the same. so far as is applicable, as those of the Supreme Court of the Cape Colony; and all criminal cases that would, if the same had been tried by a Resident Magistrate in the said Colony, be liable to review by a Judge of the Supreme Court, shall be liable to review by the Judge.

In civil cases between native and native the said courts shall decide the said cases in accordance with native law, in so far as the said law is not repugnant to principles of morality, or to any law or ordinance in force in the said territories ; provided that in any suit in which the effect of any marriage contracted according to native law or custom shall be involved, such marriage may be recognised and regarded as in all civil respects and for all civil purposes a valid marriage, though polygamous, in so far as such polygamous marriages are recognised by native law or custom. In all civil cases between natives, any Magistrate or the Judge may call to his assistance two native assessors to advise him upon native law and customs, but the decision of the case shall be vested in the Magistrate or Judge alone.

The Magistrates shall be appointed by the Company, with the approval of the High Commissioner, and shall thereupon enter on office, but the appointment shall be subject to confirmation by the Secretary of State. The Magistrates may be removed either by the Secretary of State or by the Company with the approval of the Secretary of State.

The rights of the natives are carefully safeguarded by several provisions, from which I may
quote the following :—

Fines levied upon native chiefs or tribes for
misconduct or rebellion may only be imposed
by the Administrator in Council, and every such
case shall be forthwith reported to the High
Commissioner.

Natives shall not be subjected to any exceptional legislation save as regards liquor, arms,
and ammunition, and as regards the title and
occupation of land as hereinafter referred to,
and as regards any other matter which the
Administrator in Council may with the approval
of the High Commissioner and the assent of the
Secretary of State subsequently by regulation
define ; provided that nothing herein contained
shall prevent a hut-tax being imposed by legislative authority in respect of the occupation of
huts by natives.

A Commission shall be appointed to deal
with all questions as to native settlements in
Matabeleland ; it shall be called the ' Land
Commission,' and shall be composed of three

Salisbury in the mid-1890s. Top: Pioneer Street, 1894.
Centre: early government buildings. Bottom: a new
bungalow being built by Messrs "Skipper" Hoste and
Tyndale-Biscoe

Bulawayo in the later 1890s, looking south-east. Pictured are the Mines Office, Charter Hotel, the Stock Exchange and the Post Office

persons, namely, the Judge, one member appointed by the Secretary of State, and one member appointed by the Company. Any decision of the Commission shall be subject to revision by the Secretary of State. The Land Commission shall continue for such time as may be approved by the Secretary of State after consultation with the Company, after which time all the powers and duties of the said Commission shall be vested in the Judge alone.

(Clause 27.) The Land Commission shall assign to the natives now inhabiting Matabeleland land sufficient and suitable for their agricultural and grazing requirements, and cattle sufficient for their needs. If the Company shall require any of the land thus assigned to natives for the purpose of mineral development, for sites for townships or any public works, then upon application to the Land Commission, and upon good and sufficient cause being shown, the Commission may order the land so required to be given up, and assign to the natives concerned just compensation in land elsewhere, situate in as convenient a position as possible and as far

as possible of equal suitability for their requirements in other respects.

No removal of natives from any kraal, or
from any portion of land assigned by the Land
Commission, shall take place to another locality
except after due inquiry made upon the spot,
and with the authority of the said Commission.

Natives shall have the right to acquire and
hold and dispose of landed property in the same
manner as persons who are not natives, and in
all respects such property shall be liable in the
usual manner for any obligations for which such
natives may be liable. But these provisions
shall not apply to land assigned to them by
the Land Commission under Clause 27 ; and no
contract for alienating or encumbering a native's
land shall be valid unless it is made before a
Magistrate and attested by him, after satisfying
himself that the native understands the bargain.

The above regulations appear to be fair
enough to both white and black in Matabeleland. While, on the one hand, the protection
of the natives is amply secured, on the other
hand there has been no creation of Kaffir re-

serves, and the settlers have not been restricted
in their dealings with the land in the various
ways advocated by certain well-meaning but
misguided faddists at home. While the terms
of settlement were being discussed in England,
Dr. Jameson, after consultation with Mr.
Rhodes, to some extent anticipated its provisions in so far as the treatment of the
natives and the disposition of their lands were
concerned. He took certain steps which I have
described in a previous chapter, and which the
circumstances of the case had rendered indis-
pensable, for the Matabele were naturally unwilling to cultivate their land before some
arrangement had been made as to their future,
and a famine on a large scale might have been
the result of delay in coming to an understand-
ing with them. The policy then adopted by
Dr. Jameson has since been ratified in every
respect in the Agreement between the Company
and the Imperial Government.

The scheme of administration instituted by
the Imperial Government is probably open to
the objection that it is in some respects even too

perfect, as being before its time. The machinery for government is to be more cumbersome and on a larger scale than is needed in a new country. A simpler and rougher machinery would have worked equally well until the territory had been much further developed. But, as it is, the Chartered Company, which has to pay all the salaries of Judge, Magistrates and other officials, as well as the costs of the Land Commission, and of any inquiry which the Secretary of State may think it necessary to institute into the administration or judicial system established in the country, will be saddled with a large and in some respects quite unnecessary expenditure.

Clause 34 is the only one in the Agreement to which I heard really serious objection made while I was in the Company's territory. It runs thus :—' Persons who may be appointed to such offices as may be designated in a proclamation or proclamations by the High Commissioner shall not (except in the case of an acting appointment) have any interest, either direct or indirect, in the commercial undertakings or shares of the Company. The offices to be designated in the said proclamations shall be such as may be agreed upon by the Secretary of State after consultation with the Company.'

Now it is difficult to see why a Magistrate resident in Matabeleland may not be permitted, like other people, to have a stake in its fortunes. Nearly everyone in a new country is in a position to gauge the prospects of local enterprise and engage advantageously in legitimate speculation. If the Company's officials are to be prevented from doing so, the Company will be compelled to pay higher salaries than it does now, to secure the services of capable men. An unjust and quite needless hardship will have been inflicted on the Company's present Magistrates— a well-selected body of English gentlemen, who perform their by no means easy duties with zeal, tact, and integrity—if they are compelled, under penalty of forfeiting their posts, to sell the Company's shares, which, confident in the future prosperity of the territory, they have held from the beginning. There are probably some among them who would adopt the former alternative.

In concluding this little book I will repeat that there appears to be nothing now to prevent the rapid development of this region. The country is well-administered. The Company's mining and other laws have been wisely framed and are fair to all; the difficulties of communication have been almost overcome; while the numerous opportunities for profitable enterprise having a last been realised, the capital that was so much needed is flowing into Rhodesia.

The position of the Chartered Company should now be very secure. It is earning an ever-increasing revenue from trading licenses and other sources—each canteen license, for example, costs 100l. a year. Of the amount realised by the sale of township stands I have already spoken. The hut tax will in time be levied throughout the entire territory, and this should produce a very large yearly sum; on the 60,000 huts in the Victoria district alone the tax will bring in 30,000l. per annum. Lord Grey is of opinion that next year's revenue will more than pay for the cost of administration. All the proceeds from the sale of land and from the mineral rights will therefore be available for dividends. It is, of course, impossible to esti mate the value of the Chartered Company's large interest in the mining properties that may be floated in Rhodesia, but it will be very great should the auriferous reefs fulfil their promise.

Mr. Rhodes will now have his reward in beholding a prosperous community of his fellow countrymen in occupation of this rich territory, which, by his foresight, determination, statesmanship, and strife for years with opponents at home and abroad, he has secured to Great Britain. It should always be remembered that, had it not been for his untiring vigilance, this vast high plateau, with its gold and its wealth of pastoral and arable lands, would ere this have fallen into the hands of one or other of the three foreign Powers which keenly contested its possession with the Premier of the Cape Colony.

PRINTED BY
SPOTTISWOODE AND CO., NEW-STREET SQUARE
LONDON

MESSRS. LONGMANS, GREEN, & CO.'S
CLASSIFIED CATALOGUE

OF

WORKS IN GENERAL LITERATURE.

History, Politics, Polity, Political Memoirs, &c.

Abbott.—A HISTORY OF GREECE. By EVELYN ABBOTT, M.A., LL.D.
Part I.—From the Earliest Times to the Ionian Revolt. Crown 8vo., 10s. 6d.
Part II.—500-445 B.C. Cr. 8vo., 10s. 6d.

Acland and Ransome.—A HANDBOOK IN OUTLINE OF THE POLITICAL HISTORY OF ENGLAND TO 1890. Chronologically Arranged. By the Right Hon. A. H. DYKE ACLAND, M.P., and CYRIL RANSOME, M.A. Crown 8vo., 6s.

ANNUAL REGISTER (THE). A Review of Public Events at Home and Abroad, for the year 1893. 8vo., 18s.

Volumes of the ANNUAL REGISTER for the years 1863-1892 can still be had. 18s. each.

Armstrong.—ELIZABETH FARNESE; The Termagant of Spain. By EDWARD ARMSTRONG, M.A., Fellow of Queen's College, Oxford. 8vo., 16s.

Arnold.—Works by T. ARNOLD, D.D., formerly Head Master of Rugby School.
INTRODUCTORY LECTURES ON MODERN HISTORY. 8vo., 7s. 6d.
MISCELLANEOUS WORKS. 8vo., 7s. 6d.

Bagwell.—IRELAND UNDER THE TUDORS. By RICHARD BAGWELL, LL.D. 3 vols. Vols. I. and II. From the first Invasion of the Northmen to the year 1578. 8vo., 32s. Vol. III. 1578-1603. 8vo., 18s.

Ball.—HISTORICAL REVIEW OF THE LEGISLATIVE SYSTEMS OPERATIVE IN IRELAND, from the Invasion of Henry the Second to the Union (1172-1800). By the Rt. Hon. J. T. BALL. 8vo., 6s.

Besant.—THE HISTORY OF LONDON. By WALTER BESANT. With 74 Illustrations. Crown 8vo., 1s. 9d. Or bound as a School Prize Book, 2s. 6d.

Brassey.—PAPERS AND ADDRESSES. By LORD BRASSEY. *Naval and Maritime.* 2 vols. Crown 8vo., 10s.

Bright.—A HISTORY OF ENGLAND. By the Rev. J. FRANK BRIGHT, D.D.,
Period I. MEDIÆVAL MONARCHY: The Departure of the Romans to Richard III. A.D. 449 to 1485. Crown 8vo., 4s. 6d.
Period II. PERSONAL MONARCHY: Henry VII. to James II. 1485 to 1688. Crown 8vo., 5s.
Period III. CONSTITUTIONAL MONARCHY: William and Mary, to William IV. 1689 to 1837. Crown 8vo., 7s. 6d.
Period IV. THE GROWTH OF DEMOCRACY: Victoria. 1837 to 1880. Cr. 8vo., 6s.

Buckle.—HISTORY OF CIVILISATION IN ENGLAND AND FRANCE, SPAIN AND SCOTLAND. By HENRY THOMAS BUCKLE. 3 vols. Crown 8vo., 24s.

Creighton.—HISTORY OF THE PAPACY DURING THE REFORMATION. By MANDELL CREIGHTON, D.D., LL.D., Bishop of Peterborough. Vols. I. and II., 1378-1464, 32s. Vols. III. and IV., 1464-1518., 24s. Vol. V., 1517-1527, 8vo., 15s.

Curzon.—Works by the HON. GEORGE N. CURZON, M.P.
PROBLEMS OF THE FAR EAST: JAPAN, COREA, CHINA. With 2 Maps and 50 Illustrations. 8vo., 21s.
PERSIA AND THE PERSIAN QUESTION. With 9 Maps, 96 Illustrations, Appendices, and an Index. 2 vols. 8vo., 42s.

De Tocqueville.—DEMOCRACY IN AMERICA. By ALEXIS DE TOCQUEVILLE. 2 vols. Crown 8vo., 16s.

Ewald.—Works by HEINRICH EWALD, Professor in the University of Göttengen.
THE ANTIQUITIES OF ISRAEL. 8vo., 12s. 6d.
THE HISTORY OF ISRAEL. 8 vols. 8vo. Vols. I. and II., 24s. Vols. III. and IV., 21s. Vol. V., 18s. Vol. VI., 16s. Vol. VII., 21s. Vol. VIII., 18s.

History, Politics, Polity, Political Memoirs, &c.—*continued.*

Fitzpatrick.—SECRET SERVICE UNDER PITT. By W. J. FITZPATRICK, F.S.A., Author of ' Correspondence of Daniel O'Connell'. 8vo., 7*s.* 6*d.*

Freeman.—THE HISTORICAL GEOGRAPHY OF EUROPE. By EDWARD A. FREEMAN, D.C.L., LL.D. With 65 Maps. 2 vols. 8vo., 31*s.* 6*d.*

Froude.—Works by JAMES A. FROUDE, Regius Professor of Modern History in the University of Oxford.

THE HISTORY OF ENGLAND, from the Fall of Wolsey to the Defeat of the Spanish Armada.

Popular Edition. 12 vols. Crown 8vo., 3*s.* 6*d.* each.

Silver Library Edition. 12 vols. Crown 8vo., 3*s.* 6*d.* each

THE DIVORCE OF CATHERINE OF ARAGON: the Story as told by the Imperial Ambassadors resident at the Court of Henry VIII. *In usum Laicorum.* Crown 8vo., 6*s.*

THE SPANISH STORY OF THE ARMADA, and other Essays, Historical and Descriptive. Crown 8vo., 6*s.*

THE ENGLISH IN IRELAND IN THE EIGHTEENTH CENTURY. 3 vols. Cr. 8vo., 18*s.*

SHORT STUDIES ON GREAT SUBJECTS. 4 vols. Cr. 8vo., 3*s.* 6*d.* each.

CÆSAR: a Sketch. Cr. 8vo., 3*s.* 6*d.*

Gardiner.—Works by SAMUEL RAWSON GARDINER, M.A., Hon. LL.D., Edinburgh.

HISTORY OF ENGLAND, from the Accession of James I. to the Outbreak of the Civil War, 1603-1642. 10 vols. Crown 8vo., 6*s.* each.

HISTORY OF THE GREAT CIVIL WAR, 1642-1649. 4 vols. Cr. 8vo., 6*s.* each.

HISTORY OF THE COMMONWEALTH AND THE PROTECTORATE, 1649-1660. Vol. I., 1649-1651. 8vo., 21*s.*

THE STUDENT'S HISTORY OF ENGLAND, With 378 Illustrations. Cr. 8vo., 12*s.*

Also in Three Volumes.

Vol. I. B.C. 55—A.D. 1509. With 173 Illustrations. Crown 8vo. 4*s.*

Vol. II. 1509-1689. With 96 Illustrations. Crown 8vo. 4*s.*

Vol. III. 1689-1885. With 109 Illustrations. Crown 8vo. 4*s.*

Greville.—A JOURNAL OF THE REIGNS OF KING GEORGE IV., KING WILLIAM IV., AND QUEEN VICTORIA. By CHARLES C. F. GREVILLE, formerly Clerk of the Council. 8 vols. Crown 8vo., 6*s.* each.

Hart.—PRACTICAL ESSAYS IN AMERICAN GOVERNMENT. By ALBERT BUSHNELL HART, Ph.D., &c. Editor of ' Epochs of American History,' &c., &c. Crown 8vo., 6*s.*

Hearn.—THE GOVERNMENT OF ENGLAND: its Structure and its Development By W. EDWARD HEARN. 8vo., 16*s.*

Historic Towns.—Edited by E. A. FREEMAN, D.C.L., and Rev. WILLIAM HUNT, M.A. With Maps and Plans. Crown 8vo., 3*s.* 6d. each.

BRISTOL. By the Rev. W. HUNT.
CARLISLE. By MANDELL CREIGHTON, D.D., Bishop of Peterborough.
CINQUE PORTS. By MONTAGU BURROWS.
COLCHESTER. By Rev. E. L. CUTTS.
EXETER. By E. A. FREEMAN.
LONDON. By Rev. W. J. LOFTIE.
OXFORD. By Rev. C. W. BOASE.
WINCHESTER. By Rev. G. W. KITCHIN, D.D.
YORK. By Rev. JAMES RAINE.
NEW YORK. By THEODORE ROOSEVELT.
BOSTON (U.S.) By HENRY CABOT LODGE.

Joyce.—A SHORT HISTORY OF IRELAND, from the Earliest Times to 1608. By P. W. JOYCE, LL.D. Crown 8vo., 10*s.* 6*d.*

Lang.—ST. ANDREWS. By ANDREW LANG. With 8 Plates and 24 Illustrations in the Text, by T. HODGE. 8vo., 15*s.* net.

Lecky.—Works by WILLIAM EDWARD HARTPOLE LECKY.

HISTORY OF ENGLAND IN THE EIGHTEENTH CENTURY.

Library Edition. 8 vols. 8vo., £7 4*s.*
Cabinet Edition. ENGLAND. 7 vols. Cr. 8vo., 6*s.* each. IRELAND. 5 vols. Crown 8vo., 6*s.* each.

HISTORY OF EUROPEAN MORALS FROM AUGUSTUS TO CHARLEMAGNE. 2 vols. Crown 8vo., 16*s.*

HISTORY OF THE RISE AND INFLUENCE OF THE SPIRIT OF RATIONALISM IN EUROPE. 2 vols. Crown 8vo., 16*s.*

History, Politics, Polity, Political Memoirs, &c.—*continued.*

Lecky.—Works by WILLIAM EDWARD HARTPOLE LECKY—*continued.*

THE EMPIRE : its Value and its Growth. An Inaugural Address delivered at the Imperial Institute, November 20, 1893, under the Presidency of H. R. H. the Prince of Wales. Crown 8vo. 1*s.* 6*d.*

Macaulay.—Works by LORD MACAULAY.

COMPLETE WORKS.

Cabinet Ed. 16 vols. Pt. 8vo., £4 16*s.*
Library Edition. 8 vols. 8vo., £5 5*s.*

HISTORY OF ENGLAND FROM THE ACCESSION OF JAMES THE SECOND.

Popular Edition. 2 vols. Cr. 8vo., 5*s.*
Student's Edition. 2 vols. Cr. 8vo., 12*s.*
People's Edition. 4 vols. Cr. 8vo., 16*s.*
Cabinet Edition. 8 vols. Pt. 8vo., 48*s.*
Library Edition. 5 vols. 8vo., £4.

CRITICAL AND HISTORICAL ESSAYS, WITH LAYS OF ANCIENT ROME, in 1 volume.

Popular Edition. Crown 8vo., 2*s.* 6*d.*
Authorised Edition. Crown 8vo., 2*s.* 6*d.*, or 3*s.* 6*d.*, gilt edges.
Silver Library Edition. Crown 8vo., 3*s.* 6*d.*

CRITICAL AND HISTORICAL ESSAYS.

Student's Edition. 1 vol. Cr. 8vo., 6*s.*
People's Edition. 2 vols. Cr. 8vo., 8*s.*
Trevelyan Edition. 2 vols. Cr. 8vo., 9*s.*
Cabinet Edition. 4 vols. Post 8vo., 24*s.*
Library Edition. 3 vols. 8vo., 36*s.*

ESSAYS which may be had separately, price 6*d.* each sewed, 1*s.* each cloth.

Addison and Walpole.	Lord Clive.
Frederick the Great.	The Earl of Chatham (Two Essays).
Lord Bacon.	Ranke and Gladstone.
Croker's Boswell's Johnson.	Milton and Machiavelli.
Hallam's Constitutional History.	Lord Byron, and The Comic Dramatists of the Restoration.
Warren Hastings (3*d.* swd., 6*d.* cl.).	

MISCELLANEOUS WRITINGS AND SPEECHES.

Popular Edition. Cr. 8vo., 2*s.* 6*d.*
Cabinet Edition. Including Indian Penal Code, Lays of Ancient Rome, and Miscellaneous Poems. 4 vols. Post 8vo., 24*s.*

Macaulay.—Works by LORD MACAULAY.—*continued.*

MISCELLANEOUS WRITINGS.

People's Ed. 1 vol. Cr. 8vo., 4*s.* 6*d.*
Library Edition. 2 vols. 8vo., 21*s.*

SELECTIONS FROM THE WRITINGS OF LORD MACAULAY. Edited, with Occasional Notes, by the Right Hon. Sir G. O. Trevelyan, Bart. Crown 8vo., 6*s.*

May.—THE CONSTITUTIONAL HISTORY OF ENGLAND since the Accession of George III. 1760-1870. By Sir THOMAS ERSKINE MAY, K.C.B. (Lord Farnborough). 3 vols. Crown 8vo., 18*s.*

Merivale.—Works by the Very Rev. CHARLES MERIVALE, late Dean of Ely.

HISTORY OF THE ROMANS UNDER THE EMPIRE.
Cabinet Edition. 8 vols. Cr. 8vo., 48*s.*
Silver Library Edition. 8 vols. Cr. 8vo., 3*s.* 6*d.* each.

THE FALL OF THE ROMAN REPUBLIC : a Short History of the Last Century of the Commonwealth. 12mo., 7*s.* 6*d.*

Montague.—THE ELEMENTS OF ENGLISH CONSTITUTIONAL HISTORY, from the Earliest Time to the Present Day. By F. C. MONTAGUE, M.A. Crown 8vo., 3*s.* 6*d.*

O'Brien.—IRISH IDEAS. REPRINTED ADDRESSES. By WILLIAM O'BRIEN, M.P. Cr. 8vo. 2*s.* 6*d.*

Prendergast.—IRELAND FROM THE RESTORATION TO THE REVOLUTION, 1660-1690. By JOHN P. PRENDERGAST, Author of ' The Cromwellian Settlement in Ireland '. 8vo., 5*s.*

Seebohm.—THE ENGLISH VILLAGE COMMUNITY Examined in its Relations to the Manorial and Tribal Systems, &c. By FREDERIC SEEBOHM. With 13 Maps and Plates. 8vo., 16*s.*

Sharpe.—LONDON AND THE KINGDOM : a History derived mainly from the Archives at Guildhall in the custody of the Corporation of the City of London. By REGINALD R. SHARPE, D.C.L., Records Clerk in the Office of the Town Clerk of the City of London. 3 vols. 8vo. Vols. I. and II., 10*s.* 6*d.* each.

History, Politics, Polity, Political Memoirs, &c.—*continued.*

Sheppard.—MEMORIALS OF ST. JAMES'S PALACE. By the Rev. EDGAR SHEPPARD, M.A., Sub-Dean of the Chapels Royal. With 41 Plates and 32 Illustrations in the Text. 2 Vols. 8vo, 36s. net.

Smith.—CARTHAGE AND THE CARTHAGINIANS. By R. BOSWORTH SMITH, M.A., Assistant Master in Harrow School. With Maps, Plans, &c. Cr. 8vo., 3s. 6d.

Stephens.—A HISTORY OF THE FRENCH REVOLUTION. By H. MORSE STEPHENS, Balliol College, Oxford. 3 vols. 8vo. Vols. I. and II. 18s. each.

Stubbs.—HISTORY OF THE UNIVERSITY OF DUBLIN, from its Foundation to the End of the Eighteenth Century. By J. W. STUBBS. 8vo., 12s. 6d.

Sutherland.—THE HISTORY OF AUSTRALIA AND NEW ZEALAND, from 1606 to 1890. By ALEXANDER SUTHERLAND, M.A., and GEORGE SUTHERLAND, M.A. Crown 8vo., 2s. 6d.

Todd.—PARLIAMENTARY GOVERNMENT IN THE BRITISH COLONIES. By ALPHEUS TODD, LL.D. 8vo., 30s. net.

Wakeman and Hassall.—ESSAYS INTRODUCTORY TO THE STUDY OF ENGLISH CONSTITUTIONAL HISTORY. Edited by HENRY OFFLEY WAKEMAN, M.A., and ARTHUR HASSALL, M.A. Crown 8vo., 6s.

Walpole.—Works by SPENCER WALPOLE.

HISTORY OF ENGLAND FROM THE CONCLUSION OF THE GREAT WAR IN 1815 TO 1858. 6 vols. Cr. 8vo., 6s. each.

THE LAND OF HOME RULE: being an Account of the History and Institutions of the Isle of Man. Cr. 8vo., 6s.

Wylie.—HISTORY OF ENGLAND UNDER HENRY IV. By JAMES HAMILTON WYLIE, M.A., one of H. M. Inspectors of Schools. 3 vols. Crown 8vo. Vol. I., 1399-1404, 10s. 6d. Vol. II. 15s. Vol. III. [*In preparation.*

Biography, Personal Memoirs, &c.

Armstrong.—THE LIFE AND LETTERS OF EDMUND J. ARMSTRONG. Edited by G. F. ARMSTRONG. Fcp. 8vo., 7s. 6d.

Bacon.—LETTERS AND LIFE OF FRANCIS BACON, INCLUDING ALL HIS OCCASIONAL WORKS. Edited by J. SPEDDING. 7 vols. 8vo., £4 4s.

Bagehot.—BIOGRAPHICAL STUDIES. By WALTER BAGEHOT. 8vo., 12s.

Boyd.—TWENTY-FIVE YEARS OF ST. ANDREWS, 1865-1890. By A. K. H. BOYD, D.D., LL.D., Author of ' Recreations of a Country Parson,' &c. 2 vols. 8vo. Vol. I., 12s. Vol. II., 15s.

Carlyle.—THOMAS CARLYLE: a History of his Life. By J. A. FROUDE. 1795-1835. 2 vols. Crown 8vo., 7s. 1834-1881. 2 vols. Crown 8vo., 7s.

Erasmus.—LIFE AND LETTERS OF ERASMUS: a Series of Lectures delivered at Oxford. By JAMES ANTHONY FROUDE. Crown 8vo., 6s.

Fabert.—ABRAHAM FABERT: Governor of Sedan and Marshal of France. His Life and Times, 1599-1662. By GEORGE HOOPER. With a Portrait. 8vo., 10s. 6d.

Fox.—THE EARLY HISTORY OF CHARLES JAMES FOX. By the Right Hon. Sir G. O. TREVELYAN, Bart.

Library Edition. 8vo., 18s.

Cabinet Edition. Crown 8vo., 6s.

Granville.—THE LETTERS OF HARRIET COUNTESS GRANVILLE, 1810-1845. Edited by her Son, the Hon. F. LEVESON GOWER. 2 vols. 8vo., 32s.

Hamilton.—LIFE OF SIR WILLIAM HAMILTON. By R. P. GRAVES. 3 vols. 15s. each. ADDENDUM. 8vo., 6d. sewed.

Havelock.—MEMOIRS OF SIR HENRY HAVELOCK, K.C.B. By JOHN CLARK MARSHMAN. Crown 8vo., 3s. 6d.

Macaulay.—THE LIFE AND LETTERS OF LORD MACAULAY. By the Right Hon. Sir G. O. TREVELYAN, Bart.

Popular Edition. 1 vol. Cr. 8vo., 2s. 6d.

Student's Edition. 1 vol. Cr. 8vo., 6s.

Cabinet Edition. 2 vols. Post 8vo., 12s.

Library Edition. 2 vols. 8vo., 36s.

Biography, Personal Memoirs, &c.—*continued.*

Marbot.—THE MEMOIRS OF THE BARON DE MARBOT. Translated from the French by ARTHUR JOHN BUTLER, M.A. Crown 8vo., 7s. 6d.

Montrose.—DEEDS OF MONTROSE: THE MEMOIRS OF JAMES, MARQUIS OF MONTROSE, 1639-1650. By the Rev. GEORGE WISHART, D.D. (Bishop of Edinburgh, 1662-1671). Translated by the Rev. ALEXANDER MURDOCH, F.S.A. and H. F. MORELAND SIMPSON, 4to., 36s. net.

Seebohm.—THE OXFORD REFORMERS —JOHN COLET, ERASMUS AND THOMAS MORE : a History of their Fellow-Work. By FREDERIC SEEBOHM. 8vo., 14s.

Shakespeare.—OUTLINES OF THE LIFE OF SHAKESPEARE. By J. O. HALLIWELL-PHILLIPPS. With numerous Illustrations and Fac-similes. 2 vols. Royal 8vo., £1 1s.

Shakespeare's TRUE LIFE. By JAS. WALTER. With 500 Illustrations by GERALD E. MOIRA. Imp. 8vo., 21s.

Sherbrooke.—LIFE AND LETTERS OF THE RIGHT HON. ROBERT LOWE, VISCOUNT SHERBROOKE, G.C.B., By A. PATCHETT MARTIN. With 5 Portraits. 2 vols. 8vo., 36s.

Stephen.—ESSAYS IN ECCLESIASTICAL BIOGRAPHY. By Sir JAMES STEPHEN. Crown 8vo., 7s. 6d.

Verney.—MEMOIRS OF THE VERNEY FAMILY DURING THE CIVIL WAR. Compiled from the Letters and Illustrated by the Portraits at Claydon House, Bucks. By FRANCES PARTHENOPE VERNEY. With a Preface by S. R. GARDINER, M.A., LL.D. With 38 Portraits, Woodcuts and Fac-simile. Vols. I. and II. Royal 8vo., 42s.
[Vol. III. *In the Press.*

Walford.—TWELVE ENGLISH AUTHORESSES. By L. B. WALFORD. Crown 8vo., 4s. 6d.

Wellington.—LIFE OF THE DUKE OF WELLINGTON. By the Rev. G. R. GLEIG, M.A. Crown 8vo., 3s. 6d.

Travel and Adventure, the Colonies, &c.

Arnold.—Works by Sir EDWIN ARNOLD, K.C.I.E.

SEAS AND LANDS. With 71 Illustrations. Cr. 8vo., 7s. 6d. Cheap Edition. Cr. 8vo., 3s. 6d.

WANDERING WORDS : Reprinted from Papers published in *The Daily Telegraph* and Foreign Journals and Magazines. With 45 Illustrations. 8vo., 18s.

AUSTRALIA AS IT IS, or Facts and Features, Sketches and Incidents of Australia and Australian Life, with Notices of New Zealand. By A CLERGYMAN, thirteen years resident in the interior of New South Wales. Crown 8vo., 5s.

Baker.—Works by Sir SAMUEL WHITE BAKER.

EIGHT YEARS IN CEYLON. With 6 Illustrations. Crown 8vo., 3s. 6d.

THE RIFLE AND THE HOUND IN CEYLON. 6 Illustrations. Cr. 8vo., 3s. 6d.

Bent.—Works by J. THEODORE BENT, F.S.A., F.R.G.S.

THE RUINED CITIES OF MASHONALAND : being a Record of Excavation and Exploration in 1891. With Map, 13 Plates, and 104 Illustrations in the Text. Cr. 8vo., 7s. 6d.

Bent.—Works by J. THEODORE BENT, F.S.A., F.R.G.S.—*continued.*

THE SACRED CITY OF THE ETHIOPIANS: being a Record of Travel and Research in Abyssinia in 1893. With 8 Plates and 65 Illustrations in the Text. 8vo., 18s.

Boothby.—ON THE WALLABY ; or, Through the East and Across Australia. By GUY BOOTHBY. 8vo., 18s.

Brassey.—Works by the late LADY BRASSEY.

THE LAST VOYAGE TO INDIA AND AUSTRALIA IN THE 'SUNBEAM'. With Charts and Maps, and 40 Illustrations in Monotone, and nearly 200 Illustrations in the Text. 8vo., 21s.

A VOYAGE IN THE 'SUNBEAM'; OUR HOME ON THE OCEAN FOR ELEVEN MONTHS.

Library Edition. With 8 Maps and Charts, and 118 Illustrations. 8vo., 21s.

Cabinet Edition. With Map and 66 Illustrations. Crown 8vo., 7s. 6d.

Silver Library Edition. With 66 Illustrations. Crown 8vo., 3s. 6d.

Popular Edition. With 60 Illustrations. 4to., 6d. sewed, 1s. cloth.

School Edition. With 37 Illustrations. Fcp., 2s. cloth, or 3s. white parchment.

Travel and Adventure, the Colonies, &c.—*continued.*

Brassey.—Works by the late LADY BRASSEY—*continued.*

SUNSHINE AND STORM IN THE EAST.
Library Edition. With 2 Maps and 141 Illustrations. 8vo., 21s.
Cabinet Edition. With 2 Maps and 114 Illustrations. Crown 8vo., 7s. 6d.
Popular Edition. With 103 Illustrations. 4to., 6d. sewed, 1s. cloth.
IN THE TRADES, THE TROPICS, AND THE 'ROARING FORTIES'.
Cabinet Edition. With Map and 220 Illustrations. Crown 8vo., 7s. 6d.
Popular Edition. With 183 Illustrations. 4to., 6d. sewed, 1s. cloth.
THREE VOYAGES IN THE 'SUNBEAM'.
Popular Edition.   346 Illustrations. 4to., 2s. 6d.

Bryden.—KLOOF AND KAROO: Sport, Legend, and Natural History in Cape Colony. By H. A. BRYDEN. 17 Illustrations. 8vo., 5s.

Froude.—Works by JAMES A. FROUDE.
OCEANA: or England and her Colonies. With 9 Illustrations. Crown 8vo., 2s. boards, 2s. 6d. cloth.
THE ENGLISH IN THE WEST INDIES: or the Bow of Ulysses. With 9 Illustrations. Cr. 8vo., 2s. bds., 2s. 6d. cl.

Howard.--LIFE WITH TRANS-SIBERIAN SAVAGES. By B. DOUGLAS HOWARD, M.A. Crown 8vo., 6s.

Howitt.—VISITS TO REMARKABLE PLACES, Old Halls, Battle-Fields, Scenes illustrative of Striking Passages in English History and Poetry. By WILLIAM HOWITT. With 80 Illustrations. Crown 8vo., 3s. 6d.

Knight.—Works by E. F. KNIGHT.
THE CRUISE OF THE 'ALERTE': the Narrative of a Search for Treasure on the Desert Island of Trinidad. 2 Maps and 23 Illustrations. Cr. 8vo., 3s. 6d.
WHERE THREE EMPIRES MEET: a Narrative of Recent Travel in Kashmir, Western Tibet, Baltistan, Ladak, Gilgit, and the adjoining Countries. With a Map and 54 Illustrations. Cr. 8vo., 7s. 6d.

Lees and Clutterbuck.—B. C. 1887: A RAMBLE IN BRITISH COLUMBIA. By J. A. LEES and W. J. CLUTTERBUCK, Authors of 'Three in Norway'. With Map and 75 Illustrations. Cr. 8vo., 3s. 6d.

Montague.—TALES OF A NOMAD; or, Sport and Strife. By CHARLES MONTAGUE. Crown 8vo., 6s.

Murdoch.—FROM EDINBURGH TO THE ANTARCTIC: An Artist's Notes and Sketches during the Dundee Antarctic Expedition of 1892-93. By W. G. BURN MURDOCH. With a Chapter by W. S. BRUCE, Naturalist of the Barque, "Balæna". With 2 Maps. 8vo., 18s.

Nansen.—Works by Dr. FRIDTJOF NANSEN.
THE FIRST CROSSING OF GREENLAND. With numerous Illustrations and a Map. Crown 8vo., 7s. 6d.
ESKIMO LIFE. Translated by WILLIAM ARCHER. With 31 Illustrations. 8vo., 16s.

Peary.—MY ARCTIC JOURNAL: a Year among Ice-Fields and Eskimos. By JOSEPHINE DIEBITSCH-PEARY. With 19 Plates, 3 Sketch Maps, and 44 Illustrations in the Text. 8vo., 12s.

Rockhill.—THE LAND OF THE LAMAS: Notes of a Journey through China, Mongolia, and Tibet. By WILLIAM WOODVILLE ROCKHILL. With 2 Maps and 61 Illustrations. 8vo., 15s.

Smith.—CLIMBING IN THE BRITISH ISLES. By W. P. HASKETT SMITH. With Illustrations by ELLIS CARR.
Part I. ENGLAND. Fcp. 8vo., 3s. 6d.
Part II. WALES.   [*In preparation.*
Part III. SCOTLAND. [*In preparation.*

Stephen. — THE PLAYGROUND OF EUROPE. By LESLIE STEPHEN, formerly President of the Alpine Club. New Edition, with Additions and 4 Illustrations. Crown 8vo., 6s. net.

THREE IN NORWAY. By Two of Them. With a Map and 59 Illustrations. Cr. 8vo., 2s. boards, 2s. 6d. cloth.

Von Hohnel.—DISCOVERY OF LAKES RUDOLF AND STEFANIE: A Narrative of Count SAMUEL TELEKI'S Exploring and Hunting Expedition in Eastern Equatorial Africa in 1887 and 1888. By Lieutenant LUDWIG VON HOHNEL. With 179 Illustrations and 5 Maps. 2 vols. 8vo., 42s.

Whishaw.—OUT OF DOORS IN TSARLAND; a Record of the Seeings and Doings of a Wanderer in Russia. By FRED. J. WHISHAW. Cr. 8vo., 7s. 6d.

Sport and Pastime.
THE BADMINTON LIBRARY.

Edited by the DUKE OF BEAUFORT, K.G., assisted by ALFRED E. T. WATSON.

ARCHERY. By C. J. LONGMAN and Col. H. WALROND. With Contributions by Miss LEGH and Viscount DILLON. With 195 Illustrations. Crown 8vo., 10s. 6d.

ATHLETICS AND FOOTBALL. By MONTAGUE SHEARMAN. With 51 Illlustrations. Crown 8vo., 10s. 6d.

BIG GAME SHOOTING. By C. PHILLIPPS-WOLLEY, F. C. SELOUS, ST. GEORGE LITTLEDALE, &c. With 150 Illustrations. 2 vols., 10s. 6d. each.

BOATING. By W. B. WOODGATE. With an Introduction by the Rev. EDMOND WARRE, D.D., and a Chapter on 'Rowing at Eton,' by R. HARVEY MASON. With 49 Illustrations. Cr. 8vo., 10s. 6d.

COURSING AND FALCONRY. By HARDING COX and the Hon. GERALD LASCELLES. With 76 Illustrations. Crown 8vo., 10s. 6d.

CRICKET. By A. G. STEEL and the Hon. R. H. LYTTELTON. With Contributions by ANDREW LANG, R. A. H. MITCHELL, W. G. GRACE, and F. GALE. With 64 Illustrations. Cr. 8vo., 10s. 6d.

CYCLING. By VISCOUNT BURY (Earl of Albemarle), K.C.M.G., and G. LACY HILLIER. With 89 Illustrations. Crown 8vo., 10s. 6d.

DRIVING. By the DUKE OF BEAUFORT. With 65 Illustrations. Cr. 8vo., 10s. 6d.

FENCING, BOXING. AND WRESTLING. By WALTER H. POLLOCK, F. C. GROVE. C. PREVOST, E. B. MITCHELL, and WALTER ARMSTRONG. With 42 Illustrations. Crown 8vo., 10s. 6d.

FISHING. By H. CHOLMONDELEY-PENNELL. With Contributions by the MARQUIS OF EXETER, HENRY R. FRANCIS, Major JOHN P. TRAHERNE, G. CHRISTOPHER DAVIES, R. B. MARSTON, &c.

Vol. I. Salmon, Trout, and Grayling. With 158 Illustrations. Crown 8vo., 10s. 6d.

Vol. II. Pike and other Coarse Fish. With 133 Illustrations. Crown 8vo., 10s. 6d.

GOLF. By HORACE G. HUTCHINSON, the Rt. Hon. A. J. BALFOUR, M.P., Sir W. G. SIMPSON, Bart., LORD WELLWOOD, H. S. C. EVERARD, ANDREW LANG, and other Writers. With 89 Illustrations. Crown 8vo., 10s. 6d.

HUNTING. By the DUKE OF BEAUFORT, K.G., and MOWBRAY MORRIS. With Contributions by the EARL OF SUFFOLK AND BERKSHIRE, Rev. E. W. L. DAVIES, DIGBY COLLINS, and ALFRED E. T. WATSON. With 53 Illustrations. Crown 8vo., 10s. 6d.

MOUNTAINEERING. By C. T. DENT, Sir F. POLLOCK, Bart., W. M. CONWAY, DOUGLAS FRESHFIELD, C. E. MATHEWS, &c. With 108 Illustrations. Crown 8vo., 10s. 6d.

RACING AND STEEPLE-CHASING. By the EARL OF SUFFOLK AND BERKSHIRE, W. G. CRAVEN, ARTHUR COVENTRY, &c. With 58 Illustrations. Crown 8vo., 10s. 6d.

RIDING AND POLO. By Captain ROBERT WEIR, J. MORAY BROWN, the DUKE OF BEAUFORT, K.G., the EARL of SUFFOLK AND BERKSHIRE, &c. With 59 Illustrations. Cr. 8vo., 10s. 6d.

SHOOTING. By Lord WALSINGHAM and Sir RALPH PAYNE-GALLWEY, Bart. With Contributions by LORD LOVAT, LORD C. L. KERR, and the Hon. G. LASCELLES, and A. J. STUART-WORTLEY.

Vol. I. Field and Covert. With 105 Illustrations. Crown 8vo., 10s. 6d.

Vol. II. Moor and Marsh. With 65 Illustrations. Cr. 8vo., 10s. 6d.

SKATING, CURLING, TOBOGANING, AND OTHER ICE SPORTS. By J. M. HEATHCOTE, C. G. TEBBUTT, T. MAXWELL WITHAM, the Rev. JOHN KERR, ORMOND HAKE, and Colonel BUCK With 284 Illustrations. Crown 8vo., 10s. 6d.

SWIMMING. By ARCHIBALD SINCLAIR and WILLIAM HENRY. With 119 Illustrations. Cr. 8vo., 10s. 6d.

TENNIS, LAWN TENNIS, RACQUETS, AND FIVES. By J. M. and C. G. HEATHCOTE, E. O. PLEYDELL-BOUVERIE and A. C. AINGER. With Contributions by the Hon. A. LYTTELTON, W. C. MARSHALL, Miss L. DOD, &c. With 79 Illustrations. C. 8vo., 10s. 6d.

YACHTING.

Vol. I. Cruising, Construction, Racing, Rules, Fitting-Out, &c. By Sir EDWARD SULLIVAN, Bart., LORD BRASSEY, K.C.B., C. E. SETH-SMITH, C.B., &c. With 114 Illust. Cr. 8vo., 10s. 6d.

Vol. II. Yacht Clubs. Yachting in America and the Colonies, Yacht Racing, &c. By R. T. PRITCHETT, EARL OF ONSLOW, G.C.M.G., &c With 195 Illus. Crown 8vo., 10s. 6d.

Sport and Pastime—*continued.*

FUR AND FEATHER SERIES.

Edited by A. E. T. WATSON.

THE PARTRIDGE. Natural History, by the Rev. H. A. MACPHERSON; Shooting, by A. J. STUART-WORTLEY; Cookery, by GEORGE SAINTSBURY. With 11 full-page Illustrations and Vignette by A. THORBURN, A. J. STUART-WORTLEY, and C. WHYMPER, and 15 Diagrams in the Text by A. J. STUART-WORTLEY. Crown 8vo., 5*s.*

WILDFOWL. By the Hon. JOHN SCOTT-MONTAGU, M.P., &c. Illustrated by A. J. STUART WORTLEY, A. THORBURN, and others. [*In preparation.*

THE GROUSE. Natural History by the Rev. H. A. MACPHERSON; Shooting, by A. J. STUART-WORTLEY; Cookery, by GEORGE SAINTSBURY. With 13 Illustrations by J. STUART-WORTLEY and A. THORBURN, and various Diagrams in the Text. Crown 8vo., 5*s.*

THE HARE AND THE RABBIT. By the Hon. GERALD LASCELLES, &c.
[*In preparation.*

THE PHEASANT. By A. J. STUART-WORTLEY, the Rev. H. A. MACPHERSON, and A. J. INNES SHAND.
[*In preparation.*

Campbell-Walker.—THE CORRECT CARD: or, How to Play at Whist; a Whist Catechism. By Major A. CAMPBELL-WALKER, F.R.G.S. Fcp. 8vo., 2*s.* 6*d.*

DEAD SHOT (THE): or, Sportsman's Complete Guide. Being a Treatise on the Use of the Gun, with Rudimentary and Finishing Lessons on the Art of Shooting Game of all kinds, also Game Driving, Wild-Fowl and Pigeon Shooting, Dog Breaking, etc. By MARKSMAN. Crown 8vo., 10*s.* 6*d.*

Falkener.—GAMES, ANCIENT AND ORIENTAL, AND HOW TO PLAY THEM. By EDWARD FALKENER. With numerous Photographs, Diagrams, &c. 8vo., 21*s.*

Ford.—THE THEORY AND PRACTICE OF ARCHERY. By HORACE FORD. New Edition, thoroughly Revised and Rewritten by W. BUTT, M.A. With a Preface by C. J. LONGMAN, M.A. 8vo., 14*s.*

Fowler.—RECOLLECTIONS OF OLD COUNTRY LIFE, Social, Political, Sporting, and Agricultural. By J. K. FOWLER ("Rusticus"), formerly of Aylesbury. With Portrait and 10 Illustrations. 8vo., 10*s.* 6*d.*

Francis.—A BOOK ON ANGLING: or, Treatise on the Art of Fishing in every Branch; including full Illustrated List of Salmon Flies. By FRANCIS FRANCIS. With Portrait and Coloured Plates. Cr. 8vo., 15*s.*

Hawker.—THE DIARY OF COLONEL PETER HAWKER, author of "Instructions to Young Sportsmen". With an Introduction by Sir RALPH PAYNE-GALLWEY, Bart. 2 vols. 8vo., 32*s.*

Longman.—CHESS OPENINGS. By FRED. W. LONGMAN. Fcp. 8vo., 2*s.* 6*d.*

Maskelyne.—SHARPS AND FLATS: a Complete Revelation of the Secrets of Cheating at Games of Chance and Skill. By JOHN NEVIL MASKELYNE, of the Egyptian Hall. With 62 Illustrations. Crown 8vo., 6*s.*

Payne-Gallwey. — Works by Sir RALPH PAYNE-GALLWEY, Bart.
LETTERS TO YOUNG SHOOTERS (First Series). On the Choice and Use of a Gun. With 41 Illustrations. Cr. 8vo., 7*s.* 6*d.*

LETTERS TO YOUNG SHOOTERS. (Second Series). On the Production, Preservation, and Killing of Game. With Directions in Shooting Wood-Pigeons and Breaking-in Retrievers. With a Portrait of the Author, and 103 Illustrations. Crown 8vo., 12*s.* 6*d.*

Pole.—THE THEORY OF THE MODERN SCIENTIFIC GAME OF WHIST. By W. POLE, F.R.S. Fcp. 8vo., 2*s.* 6*d.*

Proctor.—Works by R. A. PROCTOR.
HOW TO PLAY WHIST: WITH THE LAWS AND ETIQUETTE OF WHIST. Crown 8vo., 3*s.* 6*d.*
HOME WHIST: an Easy Guide to Correct Play. 16mo., 1*s.*

Ronalds.—THE FLY-FISHER'S ENTOMOLOGY. By ALFRED RONALDS. With coloured Representations of the Natural and Artificial Insect. With 20 Coloured Plates. 8vo., 14*s.*

Wilcocks. THE SEA FISHERMAN: Comprising the Chief Methods of Hook and Line Fishing in the British and other Seas, and Remarks on Nets, Boats, and Boating. By J. C. WILCOCKS. Illustrated. Crown 8vo., 6*s.*

Veterinary Medicine, &c.

Steel.—Works by JOHN HENRY STEEL,
A TREATISE ON THE DISEASES OF THE
DOG. 88 Illustrations. 8vo., 10s. 6d.
A TREATISE ON THE DISEASES OF
THE OX. With 119 Illustrations.
8vo., 15s.
A TREATISE ON THE DISEASES OF THE
SHEEP. With 100 Illustrations. 8vo.,
12s.
OUTLINES OF EQUINE ANATOMY: a
Manual for the use of Veterinary
Students in the Dissecting Room.
Crown 8vo, 7s. 6d.

Fitzwygram.--HORSES AND STABLES.
By Major-General Sir F. FITZWYGRAM,
Bart. With 56 pages of Illustrations.
8vo., 2s. 6d. net.

"Stonehenge."--THE DOG IN HEALTH
AND DISEASE. By "STONEHENGE".
With 84 Illustrations 8vo., 7s. 6d.

Youatt.—Works by WILLIAM YOUATT.
THE HORSE. With numerous Illustrations. 8vo., 7s. 6d.
THE DOG. With numerous Illustrations. 8vo., 6s.

Mental, Moral, and Political Philosophy.
LOGIC, RHETORIC, PSYCHOLOGY, ETC.

Abbott.—THE ELEMENTS OF LOGIC. By
T. K. ABBOTT, B.D. 12mo., 3s.

Aristotle.—Works by.
THE POLITICS: G. Bekker's Greek Text
of Books I., III., IV. (VII.), with an
English Translation by W. E. BOL-
LAND, M.A.; and short Introductory
Essays by A. LANG, M.A. Crown
8vo., 7s. 6d.
THE POLITICS: Introductory Essays.
By ANDREW LANG (from Bolland and
Lang's 'Politics'). Cr. 8vo., 2s. 6d.
THE ETHICS: Greek Text, Illustrated
with Essay and Notes. By Sir ALEX-
ANDER GRANT, Bart. 2 vols. 8vo.,
32s.
THE NICOMACHEAN ETHICS: Newly
Translated into English. By ROBERT
WILLIAMS. Crown 8vo., 7s. 6d.
AN INTRODUCTION TO ARISTOTLE'S
ETHICS. Books I.-IV. (Book X. c.
vi.-ix. in an Appendix.) With a con-
tinuous Analysis and Notes. By the
Rev. E. MOORE, D.D. Cr. 8vo., 10s. 6d.

Bacon.—Works by FRANCIS BACON.
COMPLETE WORKS. Edited by R. L.
ELLIS, J. SPEDDING, and D. D.
HEATH. 7 vols. 8vo., £3 13s. 6d.
LETTERS AND LIFE, including all his
occasional Works. Edited by JAMES
SPEDDING. 7 vols. 8vo., £4 4s.
THE ESSAYS: with Annotations. By
RICHARD WHATELY, D.D. 8vo.
10s. 6d.
THE ESSAYS. With Introduction, Notes,
and Index. By E. A. ABBOTT. D.D.
2 vols. Fcp. 8vo., 6s. The Text and
Index only, without Introduction and
Notes, in One Volume. Fcp. 8vo.,
2s. 6d.

Bain.—Works by ALEXANDER BAIN,
LL.D.
MENTAL SCIENCE. Crown 8vo., 6s. 6d.
MORAL SCIENCE. Crown 8vo., 4s. 6d.
*The two works as above can be had in one
volume, price 10s. 6d.*
SENSES AND THE INTELLECT. 8vo., 15s.
EMOTIONS AND THE WILL. 8vo., 15s.
LOGIC, DEDUCTIVE AND INDUCTIVE.
Part I., 4s. Part II., 6s. 6d.
PRACTICAL ESSAYS. Crown 8vo., 3s.

Bray.—Works by CHARLES BRAY.
THE PHILOSOPHY OF NECESSITY: or
Law in Mind as in Matter. Cr. 8vo., 5s.
THE EDUCATION OF THE FEELINGS: a
Moral System for Schools. Crown
8vo., 2s. 6d.

Bray.—ELEMENTS OF MORALITY, in
Easy Lessons for Home and School
Teaching. By Mrs. CHARLES BRAY.
Cr. 8vo., 1s. 6d.

Crozier.—CIVILISATION AND PRO-
GRESS. By JOHN BEATTIE CROZIER,
M.D. With New Preface, more fully
explaining the nature of the New Orga-
non used in the solution of its problems.
8vo., 14s.

Davidson.—THE LOGIC OF DEFINI-
TION, Explained and Applied. By
WILLIAM L. DAVIDSON, M.A. Crown
8vo., 6s.

Green.—THE WORKS OF THOMAS HILL
GREEN. Edited by R. L. NETTLESHIP.
Vols. I. and II. Philosophical Works.
8vo., 16s. each.
Vol. III. Miscellanies. With Index to
the three Volumes, and Memoir. 8vo.,
21s.

Mental, Moral and Political Philosophy—*continued.*

Hearn.—THE ARYAN HOUSEHOLD : its Structure and its Development. An Introduction to Comparative Jurisprudence. By W. EDWARD HEARN. 8vo., 16*s.*

Hodgson.—Works by SHADWORTH H. HODGSON.

TIME AND SPACE : a Metaphysical Essay. 8vo., 16*s.*

THE THEORY OF PRACTICE : an Ethical Inquiry. 2 vols. 8vo., 24*s.*

THE PHILOSOPHY OF REFLECTION. 2 vols. 8vo., 21*s.*

Hume.—THE PHILOSOPHICAL WORKS OF DAVID HUME. Edited by T. H. GREEN and T. H. GROSE. 4 vols. 8vo., 56*s.* Or separately, Essays. 2 vols. 28*s.* Treatise of Human Nature. 2 vols. 28*s.*

Johnstone.—A SHORT INTRODUCTION TO THE STUDY OF LOGIC. By LAURENCE JOHNSTONE. With Questions. Cr. 8vo., 2*s.* 6*d.*

Jones.—AN INTRODUCTION TO GENERAL LOGIC. By E. E. CONSTANCE JONES. Cr. 8vo., 4*s.* 6*d.*

Justinian.—THE INSTITUTES OF JUSTINIAN : Latin Text, chiefly that of Huschke, with English Introduction, Translation, Notes, and Summary. By THOMAS C. SANDARS, M.A. 8vo. 18*s.*

Kant.—Works by IMMANUEL KANT.

CRITIQUE OF PRACTICAL REASON, AND OTHER WORKS ON THE THEORY OF ETHICS. Translated by T. K. ABBOTT, B.D. With Memoir. 8vo., 12*s.* 6*d.*

INTRODUCTION TO LOGIC, AND HIS ESSAY ON THE MISTAKEN SUBTILTY OF THE FOUR FIGURES. Translated by T. K. ABBOTT, and with Notes by S. T. COLERIDGE. 8vo., 6*s.*

Killick.—HANDBOOK TO MILL'S SYSTEM OF LOGIC. By Rev. A. H. KILLICK, M.A. Crown 8vo., 3*s.* 6*d.*

Ladd.—Works by GEORGE TURNBULL LADD.

ELEMENTS OF PHYSIOLOGICAL PSYCHOLOGY. 8vo., 21*s.*

OUTLINES OF PHYSIOLOGICAL PSYCHOLOGY. A Text-Book of Mental Science for Academies and Colleges. 8vo., 12*s.*

Ladd.—Works by G. T. LADD.—*cont.*

PSYCHOLOGY, DESCRIPTIVE AND EXPLANATORY : a Treatise of the Phenomena, Laws, and Development of Human Mental Life. 8vo., 21*s.*

Lewes.—THE HISTORY OF PHILOSOPHY, from Thales to Comte. By GEORGE HENRY LEWES. 2 vols. 8vo., 32*s.*

Max Müller.—Works by F. MAX MÜLLER.

THE SCIENCE OF THOUGHT. 8vo., 21*s.*

THREE INTRODUCTORY LECTURES ON THE SCIENCE OF THOUGHT. 8vo., 2*s.* 6*d.*

Mill.—ANALYSIS OF THE PHENOMENA OF THE HUMAN MIND. By JAMES MILL. 2 vols. 8vo., 28*s.*

Mill.—Works by JOHN STUART MILL.

A SYSTEM OF LOGIC. Cr. 8vo., 3*s.* 6*d.*

ON LIBERTY. Cr. 8vo., 1*s.* 4*d.*

ON REPRESENTATIVE GOVERNMENT. Crown 8vo., 2*s.*

UTILITARIANISM. 8vo., 5*s.*

EXAMINATION OF SIR WILLIAM HAMILTON'S PHILOSOPHY. 8vo., 16*s.*

NATURE, THE UTILITY OF RELIGION, AND THEISM. Three Essays. 8vo., 5*s.*

Monck.—INTRODUCTION TO LOGIC. By W. H. S. MONCK. Crown 8vo., 5*s.*

Sidgwick.—DISTINCTION: and the Criticism of Belief. By ALFRED SIDGWICK. Crown 8vo., 6*s.*

Stock.—DEDUCTIVE LOGIC. By ST. GEORGE STOCK. Fcp. 8vo., 3*s.* 6*d.*

Sully.—Works by JAMES SULLY.

THE HUMAN MIND : a Text-book of Psychology. 2 vols. 8vo., 21*s.*

OUTLINES OF PSYCHOLOGY. 8vo., 9*s.*

THE TEACHER'S HANDBOOK OF PSYCHOLOGY. Crown 8vo., 5*s.*

Swinburne.—PICTURE LOGIC: an Attempt to Popularise the Science of Reasoning. By ALFRED JAMES SWINBURNE, M.A. With 23 Woodcuts. Post 8vo., 5*s.*

Mental, Moral and Political Philosophy—*continued.*

Thomson.—OUTLINES OF THE NECESSARY LAWS OF THOUGHT: a Treatise on Pure and Applied Logic. By WILLIAM THOMSON, D.D., formerly Lord Archbishop of York. Post 8vo., 6s.

Webb.—THE VEIL OF ISIS: a Series of Essays on Idealism. By T. E. WEBB. 8vo., 10s. 6d.

Whately.—Works by R. WHATELY, D.D.
BACON'S ESSAYS. With Annotation. By R. WHATELY. 8vo., 10s. 6d.
ELEMENTS OF LOGIC. Cr. 8vo., 4s. 6d.
ELEMENTS OF RHETORIC. Cr. 8vo., 4s. 6d.
LESSONS ON REASONING. Fcp. 8vo., 1s. 6d.

Zeller.—Works by Dr. EDWARD ZELLER, Professor in the University of Berlin.
THE STOICS, EPICUREANS, AND SCEPTICS. Translated by the Rev. O. J. REICHEL, M.A. Crown 8vo., 15s.
OUTLINES OF THE HISTORY OF GREEK PHILOSOPHY. Translated by SARAH F. ALLEYNE and EVELYN ABBOTT. Crown 8vo., 10s. 6d.
PLATO AND THE OLDER ACADEMY. Translated by SARAH F. ALLEYNE and ALFRED GOODWIN, B.A. Crown 8vo., 18s.
SOCRATES AND THE SOCRATIC SCHOOLS. Translated by the Rev. O. J. REICHEL, M.A. Crown 8vo., 10s. 6d.

MANUALS OF CATHOLIC PHILOSOPHY.
(Stonyhurst Series.)

A MANUAL OF POLITICAL ECONOMY. By C. S. DEVAS, M.A. Cr. 8vo., 6s. 6d.
FIRST PRINCIPLES OF KNOWLEDGE. By JOHN RICKABY, S.J. Crown 8vo., 5s.
GENERAL METAPHYSICS. By JOHN RICKABY, S.J. Crown 8vo., 5s.
LOGIC. By RICHARD F. CLARKE, S.J. Crown 8vo., 5s.

MORAL PHILOSOPHY (ETHICS AND NATURAL LAW). By JOSEPH RICKABY, S.J. Crown 8vo., 5s.
NATURAL THEOLOGY. By BERNARD BOEDDER, S.J. Crown 8vo., 6s. 6d.
PSYCHOLOGY. By MICHAEL MAHER, S.J. Crown 8vo., 6s. 6d.

History and Science of Language, &c.

Davidson.—LEADING AND IMPORTANT ENGLISH WORDS: Explained and Exemplified. By WILLIAM L. DAVIDSON, M.A. Fcp. 8vo., 3s. 6d.

Farrar.—LANGUAGE AND LANGUAGES. By F. W. FARRAR, D.D., F.R.S., Cr. 8vo., 6s.

Graham.—ENGLISH SYNONYMS, Classified and Explained: with Practical Exercises. By G. F. GRAHAM. Fcp. 8vo., 6s.

Max Müller.—Works by F. MAX MÜLLER.
THE SCIENCE OF LANGUAGE, Founded on Lectures delivered at the Royal Institution in 1861 and 1863. 2 vols. Crown 8vo., 21s.
BIOGRAPHIES OF WORDS, AND THE HOME OF THE ARYAS. Crown 8vo., 7s. 6d.

Max Müller.—Works by F. MAX MÜLLER—*continued.*
THREE LECTURES ON THE SCIENCE OF LANGUAGE, AND ITS PLACE IN GENERAL EDUCATION, delivered at Oxford, 1889. Crown 8vo., 3s.

Roget. — THESAURUS OF ENGLISH WORDS AND PHRASES. Classified and Arranged so as to Facilitate the Expression of Ideas and assist in Literary Composition. By PETER MARK ROGET, M.D., F.R.S. Recomposed throughout, enlarged and improved, partly from the Author's Notes, and with a full Index, by the Author's Son, JOHN LEWIS ROGET. Crown 8vo., 10s. 6d.

Whately.—ENGLISH SYNONYMS. By E. JANE WHATELY. Fcp. 8vo., 3s.

Political Economy and Economics.

Ashley.—ENGLISH ECONOMIC HISTORY AND THEORY. By W. J. ASHLEY, M.A. Crown 8vo., Part I., 5s. Part II., 10s. 6d.

Bagehot. — ECONOMIC STUDIES. By WALTER BAGEHOT. 8vo., 10s. 6d.

Barnett.—PRACTICABLE SOCIALISM : Essays on Social Reform. By the Rev. S. A. and Mrs. BARNETT. Cr. 8vo., 6s.

Brassey.—PAPERS AND ADDRESSES ON WORK AND WAGES. By Lord BRASSEY. Edited by J. POTTER, and with Introduction by GEORGE HOWELL, M.P. Crown 8vo., 5s.

Devas.—A MANUAL OF POLITICAL ECONOMY. By C. S. DEVAS, M.A. Crown 8vo., 6s. 6d. (*Manuals of Catholic Philosophy.*)

Dowell.—A HISTORY OF TAXATION AND TAXES IN ENGLAND, from the Earliest Times to the Year 1885. By STEPHEN DOWELL (4 vols. 8vo.) Vols. I. and II. The History of Taxation, 21s. Vols. III. and IV. The History of Taxes, 21s.

Jordan.—THE STANDARD OF VALUE. By WILLIAM LEIGHTON JORDAN. 8vo., 6s.

Leslie.—ESSAYS IN POLITICAL ECONOMY. By T. E. CLIFFE LESLIE. 8vo., 10s. 6d.

Macleod.—Works by HENRY DUNNING MACLEOD, M.A.
BIMETALISM. 8vo., 5s. net.
THE ELEMENTS OF BANKING. Crown 8vo., 3s. 6d.
THE THEORY AND PRACTICE OF BANKING. Vol. I. 8vo., 12s. Vol. II. 14s.
THE THEORY OF CREDIT. 8vo. Vol. I. 10s. net. Vol. II., Part I., 4s. 6d. Vol. II. Part II., 10s. 6d.

Mill.—POLITICAL ECONOMY. By JOHN STUART MILL.
Popular Edition. Crown 8vo., 3s. 6d.
Library Edition. 2 vols. 8vo , 30s.

Shirres.—AN ANALYSIS OF THE IDEAS OF ECONOMICS. By L. P. SHIRRES, B.A., sometime Finance Under-Secretary of the Government of Bengal. Crown 8vo., 6s.

Symes.—POLITICAL ECONOMY : a Short Text-book of Political Economy. With Problems for Solution, and Hints for Supplementary Reading. By Prof. J. E. SYMES, M.A., of University College, Nottingham. Crown 8vo., 2s. 6d.

Toynbee.—LECTURES ON THE INDUSTRIAL REVOLUTION OF THE 18th CENTURY IN ENGLAND. By ARNOLD TOYNBEE. With a Memoir of the Author by B. JOWETT. 8vo., 10s. 6d.

Webb.—THE HISTORY OF TRADE UNIONISM. By SIDNEY and BEATRICE WEBB. With Map and full Bibliography of the Subject. 8vo., 18s.

Wilson.—Works by A. J. WILSON. Chiefly reprinted from *The Investors' Review.*
PRACTICAL HINTS TO SMALL INVESTORS. Crown 8vo., 1s.
PLAIN ADVICE ABOUT LIFE INSURANCE. Crown 8vo., 1s.

Evolution, Anthropology, &c.

Clodd.—Works by EDWARD CLODD.
THE STORY OF CREATION : a Plain Account of Evolution. With 77 Illustrations. Crown 8vo., 3s. 6d.
A PRIMER OF EVOLUTION : being a Popular Abridged Edition of 'The Story of Creation'. With Illust. Fcp. 8vo., 1s. 6d.   [*In the Press.*

Huth.—THE MARRIAGE OF NEAR KIN, considered with Respect to the Law of Nations, the Result of Experience, and the Teachings of Biology. By ALFRED HENRY HUTH. Royal 8vo., 7s. 6d.

Lang.—CUSTOM AND MYTH : Studies of Early Usage and Belief. By ANDREW LANG, M.A. With 15 Illustrations. Crown 8vo., 3s. 6d.

Lubbock.—THE ORIGIN OF CIVILISATION and the Primitive Condition of Man. By Sir J. LUBBOCK, Bart., M.P. With 5 Plates and 20 Illustrations in the Text. 8vo. 18s.

Romanes.—Works by GEORGE JOHN ROMANES, M.A., LL.D., F.R.S.
DARWIN, AND AFTER DARWIN : an Exposition of the Darwinian Theory, and a Discussion on Post-Darwinian Questions. Part I. The Darwinian Theory. With Portrait of Darwin and 125 Illustrations. Crown 8vo., 10s. 6d.
AN EXAMINATION OF WEISMANNISM. Crown 8vo., 6s.

Classical Literature and Translations, &c.

Abbott.—HELLENICA. A Collection of Essays on Greek Poetry, Philosophy, History, and Religion. Edited by EVELYN ABBOTT, M.A., LL.D. 8vo., 16s.

Æschylus.—EUMENIDES OF ÆSCHYLUS. With Metrical English Translation. By J. F. DAVIES. 8vo., 7s.

Aristophanes.—The ACHARNIANS OF ARISTOPHANES, translated into English Verse. By R. Y. TYRRELL. Crown 8vo., 1s.

Becker.—Works by Professor BECKER.
GALLUS: or, Roman Scenes in the Time of Augustus. Illustrated. Post 8vo., 7s. 6d.

CHARICLES: or, Illustrations of the Private Life of the Ancient Greeks. Illustrated. Post 8vo., 7s. 6d.

Cicero.—CICERO'S CORRESPONDENCE. By R. Y. TYRRELL. Vols. I., II., III. 8vo., each 12s. Vol. IV., 15s.

Farnell.—GREEK LYRIC POETRY: a Complete Collection of the Surviving Passages from the Greek Song-Writing. Arranged with Prefatory Articles, Introductory Matter and Commentary. By GEORGE S. FARNELL, M.A. With 5 Plates. 8vo., 16s.

Harrison.—MYTHS OF THE ODYSSEY IN ART AND LITERATURE. By JANE E. HARRISON. Illustrated with Outline Drawings. 8vo., 18s.

Lang.—HOMER AND THE EPIC. By ANDREW LANG. Crown 8vo., 9s. net.

Mackail.—SELECT EPIGRAMS FROM THE GREEK ANTHOLOGY. By J. W. MACKAIL, Fellow of Balliol College, Oxford. Edited with a Revised Text, Introduction, Translation, and Notes. 8vo., 16s.

Plato.—PARMENIDES OF PLATO, Text, with Introduction, Analysis, &c. By T. MAGUIRE. 8vo., 7s. 6d.

Rich.—A DICTIONARY OF ROMAN AND GREEK ANTIQUITIES. By A. RICH, B.A. With 2000 Woodcuts. Crown 8vo., 7s. 6d.

Sophocles.—Translated into English Verse. By ROBERT WHITELAW, M.A., Assistant Master in Rugby School: late Fellow of Trinity College, Cambridge. Crown 8vo., 8s. 6d.

Theocritus.—THE IDYLLS OF THEOCRITUS. Translated into English Verse. By JAMES HENRY HALLARD, M.A. Oxon. Fcp. 4to., 6s. 6d.

Tyrrell.—TRANSLATIONS INTO GREEK AND LATIN VERSE. Edited by R. Y. TYRRELL. 8vo., 6s.

Virgil.—THE ÆNEID OF VIRGIL. Translated into English Verse by JOHN CONINGTON. Crown 8vo., 6s.

THE POEMS OF VIRGIL. Translated into English Prose by JOHN CONINGTON. Crown 8vo., 6s.

THE ÆNEID OF VIRGIL, freely translated into English Blank Verse. By W. J. THORNHILL. Crown 8vo., 7s. 6d.

THE ÆNEID OF VIRGIL. Books 1. to VI. Translated into English Verse by JAMES RHOADES. Crown 8vo., 5s.

Wilkins.—THE GROWTH OF THE HOMERIC POEMS. By G. WILKINS. 8vo. 6s.

Poetry and the Drama.

Allingham.—Works by WILLIAM ALLINGHAM.

IRISH SONGS AND POEMS. With Frontispiece of the Waterfall of Asaroe. Fcp. 8vo., 6s.

LAURENCE BLOOMFIELD. With Portrait of the Author. Fcp. 8vo., 3s. 6d.

FLOWER PIECES; DAY AND NIGHT SONGS; BALLADS. With 2 Designs by D. G. ROSSETTI. Fcp. 8vo., 6s.; large paper edition, 12s.

LIFE AND PHANTASY: with Frontispiece by Sir J. E. MILLAIS, Bart., and Design by ARTHUR HUGHES. Fcp. 8vo., 6s.; large paper edition, 12s.

THOUGHT AND WORD, AND ASHBY MANOR: a Play. With Portrait of the Author (1865), and four Theatrical Scenes drawn by Mr. Allingham. Fcp. 8vo., 6s.; large paper edition, 12s.

BLACKBERRIES. Imperial 16mo., 6s.

Sets of the above 6 vols. may be had in uniform half-parchment binding, price 30s.

Poetry and the Drama—*continued.*

Armstrong.—Works by G. F. Savage-
Armstrong.
Poems : Lyrical and Dramatic. Fcp.
8vo., 6s.
King Saul. (The Tragedy of Israel,
Part I.) Fcp. 8vo. 5s.
King David. (The Tragedy of Israel,
Part II.) Fcp. 8vo., 6s.
King Solomon. (The Tragedy of
Israel, Part III.) Fcp. 8vo., 6s.
Ugone : a Tragedy. Fcp. 8vo., 6s.
A Garland from Greece : Poems.
Fcp. 8vo., 7s. 6d.
Stories of Wicklow : Poems. Fcp.
8vo., 7s. 6d.
Mephistopheles in Broadcloth: a
Satire. Fcp. 8vo., 4s.
One in the Infinite : a Poem. Cr.
8vo., 7s. 6d.

Armstrong.—The Poetical Works
of Edmund J. Armstrong. Fcp.
8vo., 5s.

Arnold.—Works by Sir Edwin Arnold,
K.C.I.E., Author of 'The Light of
Asia,' &c.
The Light of the World : or, the
Great Consummation. A Poem.
Crown 8vo., 7s. 6d. net.
Presentation Edition. With 14 Illus-
trations by W. Holman Hunt.
4to., 20s. net.
Potiphar's Wife, and other Poems.
Crown 8vo., 5s. net.
Adzuma : or, the Japanese Wife. A
Play. Crown 8vo., 6s. 6d. net.

Bell.—Chamber Comedies : a Collec-
tion of Plays and Monologues for the
Drawing Room. By Mrs. Hugh
Bell. Crown 8vo., 6s.

Björnsen.—Works by Björnstjerne
Björnsen.
Pastor Sang : a Play. Translated by
William Wilson. Cr. 8vo., 5s.
A Gauntlet : a Drama. Translated
into English by Osman Edwards.
With Portrait of the Author. Crown
8vo., 5s.

Cochrane.—The Kestrel's Nest,
and other Verses. By Alfred Cochrane. Fcp. 8vo., 3s. 6d.

Dante.—La Commedia di Dante. A
New Text, carefully revised with the
aid of the most recent Editions and
Collations. Small 8vo., 6s.

Goethe.
Faust, Part I., the German Text, with
Introduction and Notes. By Albert
M. Selss, Ph.D., M.A.   Cr. 8vo., 5s.
Faust. Translated, with Notes. By
T. E. Webb. 8vo., 12s. 6d.

Ingelow.—Works by Jean Ingelow.
Poetical Works. 2 vols. Fcp. 8vo.,
12s.
Lyrical and Other Poems. Selected
from the Writings of Jean Ingelow.
Fcp. 8vo., 2s. 6d. ; cloth plain, 3s.
cloth gilt.

Kendall.—Songs from Dreamland.
By May Kendall. Fcp. 8vo., 5s. net.

Lang.—Works by Andrew Lang.
Ban and Arrière Ban. A Rally of
Fugitive Rhymes. Fcp. 8vo., 5s.
net.
Grass of Parnassus. Fcp. 8vo.,
2s. 6d. net.
Ballads of Books. Edited by
Andrew Lang. Fcp. 8vo., 6s.
The Blue Poetry Book. Edited by
Andrew Lang. With 12 Plates and
88 Illustrations in the Text by H. J.
Ford and Lancelot Speed. Crown
8vo., 6s.
*Special Edition, printed on Indian
paper. With Notes, but without
Illustrations. Crown 8vo., 7s. 6d.*

Lecky.—Poems. By W. E. H. Lecky.
Fcp. 8vo., 5s.

Leyton.—Works by Frank Leyton.
The Shadows of the Lake, and
other Poems. Crown 8vo., 7s. 6d.
Cheap Edition. Crown 8vo., 3s. 6d.
Skeleton Leaves : Poems. Crown
8vo., 6s.

Lytton.—Works by The Earl of
Lytton (Owen Meredith).
Marah. Fcp. 8vo., 6s. 6d.
King Poppy : a Fantasia. With 1
Plate and Design on Title-Page by
Sir Ed. Burne-Jones, A.R.A. Crown
8vo., 10s. 6d.
The Wanderer. Cr. 8vo., 10s. 6d.
Lucile. Crown 8vo., 10s. 6d.
Selected Poems. Cr. 8vo., 10s. 6d.

Poetry and the Drama—*continued.*

Macaulay.—LAYS OF ANCIENT ROME, &c. By Lord MACAULAY.

Illustrated by G. SCHARF. Fcp. 4to., 10s. 6d.

———————— Bijou Edition. 18mo., 2s. 6d., gilt top.

———————— Popular Edition. Fcp. 4to., 6d. sewed, 1s. cloth.

Illustrated by J. R. WEGUELIN. Crown 8vo., 3s. 6d.

Annotated Edition. Fcp. 8vo., 1s. sewed, 1s. 6d. cloth.

Nesbit.—LAYS AND LEGENDS. By E. NESBIT (Mrs. HUBERT BLAND). First Series. Crown 8vo., 3s. 6d. Second Series, with Portrait. Crown 8vo., 5s.

Piatt.—Works by SARAH PIATT.

POEMS. With portrait of the Author. 2 vols. Crown 8vo., 10s.

AN ENCHANTED CASTLE, AND OTHER POEMS : Pictures, Portraits and People in Ireland. Crown 8vo., 3s. 6d.

Piatt.—Works by JOHN JAMES PIATT.

IDYLS AND LYRICS OF THE OHIO VALLEY. Crown 8vo., 5s.

LITTLE NEW WORLD IDYLS. Cr. 8vo., 5s.

Rhoades.—TERESA AND OTHER POEMS. By JAMES RHOADES. Crown 8vo., 3s. 6d.

Riley.—Works by JAMES WHITCOMB RILEY.

OLD FASHIONED ROSES : Poems. 12mo., 5s.

POEMS HERE AT HOME. Fcap. 8vo., 6s. net.

Roberts. — SONGS OF THE COMMON DAY, AND AVE : an Ode for the Shelley Centenary. By CHARLES G. D. ROBERTS. Crown 8vo., 3s. 6d.

Shakespeare.—BOWDLER'S FAMILY SHAKESPEARE. With 36 Woodcuts. 1 vol. 8vo., 14s. Or in 6 vols. Fcp. 8vo., 21s.

THE SHAKESPEARE BIRTHDAY BOOK. By MARY F. DUNBAR. 32mo., 1s. 6d. Drawing-Room Edition, with Photographs. Fcp. 8vo., 10s. 6d.

Sturgis.—A BOOK OF SONG. By JULIAN STURGIS. 16mo., 5s.

Works of Fiction, Humour, &c.

Anstey.—Works by F. ANSTEY, Author of ' Vice Versâ '.

THE BLACK POODLE, and other Stories. Crown 8vo., 2s. boards, 2s. 6d. cloth.

VOCES POPULI. Reprinted from ' Punch '. First Series. With 20 Illustrations by J. BERNARD PARTRIDGE. Cr. 8vo., 3s. 6d.

THE TRAVELLING COMPANIONS. Reprinted from ' Punch '. With 25 Illustrations by J. BERNARD PARTRIDGE. Post 4to., 5s.

THE MAN FROM BLANKLEY'S : a Story in Scenes, and other Sketches. With 24 Illustrations by J. BERNARD PARTRIDGE. Fcp. 4to., 6s.

Astor.—A JOURNEY IN OTHER WORLDS. a Romance of the Future. By JOHN JACOB ASTOR. With 10 Illustrations. Cr. 8vo., 6s.

Baker.—BY THE WESTERN. SEA. By JAMES BAKER, Author of ' John Westacott '. Crown 8vo., 3s. 6d.

Beaconsfield.—Works by the Earl of BEACONSFIELD.

NOVELS AND TALES. Cheap Edition. Complete in 11 vols. Cr. 8vo., 1s. 6d. each.

Vivian Grey.	Henrietta Temple.
The Young Duke, &c.	Venetia. Tancred.
Alroy, Ixion, &c.	Coningsby. Sybil.
Contarini Fleming, &c.	Lothair. Endymion.

NOVELS AND TALES. The Hughenden Edition. With 2 Portraits and 11 Vignettes. 11 vols. Cr. 8vo., 42s.

Clegg.—DAVID'S LOOM : a Story of Rochdale life in the early years of the Nineteenth Century. By JOHN TRAFFORD CLEGG. Crown 8vo. 6s.

Works of Fiction, Humour, &c.—*continued.*

Deland.—Works by MARGARET DE-LAND, Author of 'John Ward'.

THE STORY OF A CHILD. Cr. 8vo., 5s.

MR. TOMMY DOVE, and other Stories. Crown 8vo., 6s.

PHILIP AND HIS WIFE. Cr. 8vo., 6s.

Dougall.—Works by L. DOUGALL.

BEGGARS ALL. Crown 8vo., 3s. 6d.

WHAT NECESSITY KNOWS. Crown 8vo., 6s.

Doyle.—Works by A. CONAN DOYLE.

MICAH CLARKE: a Tale of Monmouth's Rebellion. With Frontispiece and Vignette. Cr. 8vo., 3s. 6d.

THE CAPTAIN OF THE POLESTAR, and other Tales. Cr. 8vo., 3s. 6d.

THE REFUGEES: a Tale of Two Continents. Cr. 8vo., 6s.

Farrar.—DARKNESS AND DAWN: or, Scenes in the Days of Nero. An Historic Tale. By Archdeacon FARRAR. Cr. 8vo., 7s. 6d.

Forster.—MAJOR JOSHUA. By FRANCIS FORSTER. Crown 8vo., 6s.

Froude.—THE TWO CHIEFS OF DUNBOY: an Irish Romance of the Last Century. By J. A. FROUDE. Cr. 8vo., 3s. 6d.

Gilkes. — THE THING THAT HATH BEEN: or, a Young Man's Mistake. By A. H. GILKES, M.A., Master of Dulwich College, Author of 'Boys and Masters'. Crown 8vo., 6s.

Haggard.—Works by H. RIDER HAGGARD.

SHE. With 32 Illustrations. Crown 8vo., 3s. 6d.

ALLAN QUATERMAIN. With 31 Illustrations. Crown 8vo., 3s. 6d.

MAIWA'S REVENGE; or, The War of the Little Hand. Cr. 8vo., 1s. boards, 1s. 6d. cloth.

COLONEL QUARITCH, V.C. Cr. 8vo., 3s. 6d.

CLEOPATRA. With 29 Illustrations Crown 8vo., 3s. 6d.

BEATRICE. Cr. 8vo., 3s. 6d.

Haggard.—Works by H. RIDER HAGGARD—*continued.*

ERIC BRIGHTEYES. With 51 Illustrations. Cr. 8vo., 3s. 6d.

NADA THE LILY. With 23 Illustrations. Cr. 8vo., 6s.

MONTEZUMA'S DAUGHTER. With 24 Illustrations. Crown 8vo., 6s.

ALLAN'S WIFE. With 34 Illustrations. Crown 8vo., 3s. 6d.

THE WITCH'S HEAD. With 16 Illustrations. Crown 8vo., 3s. 6d.

MR. MEESON'S WILL. With 16 Illustrations. Crown 8vo., 3s. 6d.

DAWN. With 16 Illustrations. Crown 8vo., 3s. 6d.

THE PEOPLE OF THE MIST. With 16 Illustrations. Cr. 8vo., 6s.

Haggard and Lang.—THE WORLD'S DESIRE. By H. RIDER HAGGARD and ANDREW LANG. With 27 Illustrations by M. GREIFFENHAGEN. Cr. 8vo., 3s. 6d.

Harte. — IN THE CARQUINEZ WOODS, and other Stories. By BRET HARTE. Cr. 8vo., 3s. 6d.

Hornung.—THE UNBIDDEN GUEST. By E. W. HORNUNG. Crown 8vo., 6s.

Lyall.—Works by EDNA LYALL, Author of 'Donovan,' &c.

THE AUTOBIOGRAPHY OF A SLANDER. Fcp. 8vo., 1s. sewed.

Presentation Edition. With 20 Illustrations by LANCELOT SPEED. Cr. 8vo., 2s. 6d. net.

DOREEN: The Story of a Singer. Cr. 8vo., 6s.

Melville.—Works by G. J. WHYTE MELVILLE.

The Gladiators.	Holmby House.
The Interpreter.	Kate Coventry.
Good for Nothing.	Digby Grand.
The Queen's Maries.	General Bounce.

Cr. 8vo., 1s. 6d. each.

Oliphant.—Works by Mrs. OLIPHANT.

MADAM. Cr. 8vo., 1s. 6d.

IN TRUST. Cr. 8vo., 1s. 6d.

Parr.—CAN THIS BE LOVE? By Mrs. PARR, Author of 'Dorothy Fox'. Cr. 8vo., 6s.

Works of Fiction, Humour, &c.—*continued.*

Payn.—Works by JAMES PAYN.
THE LUCK OF THE DARRELLS. Cr. 8vo., 1s. 6d.
THICKER THAN WATER. Cr. 8vo., 1s. 6d.

Phillipps-Wolley.—SNAP: a Legend of the Lone Mountain. By C. PHIL-LIPPS-WOLLEY. With 13 Illustrations by H. G. WILLINK. Cr. 8vo., 3s. 6d.

Sewell.—Works by ELIZABETH M. SEWELL.

A Glimpse of the World.	Amy Herbert.
Laneton Parsonage.	Cleve Hall.
Margaret Percival.	Gertrude.
Katharine Ashton.	Home Life.
The Earl's Daughter.	After Life.
The Experience of Life.	Ursula. Ivors.

Cr. 8vo., 1s. 6d. each cloth plain. 2s. 6d. each cloth extra, gilt edges.

Stevenson.—Works by ROBERT LOUIS STEVENSON.
STRANGE CASE OF DR. JEKYLL AND MR. HYDE. Fcp. 8vo., 1s. sewed. 1s. 6d. cloth.
THE DYNAMITER. Fcp. 8vo., 1s. sewed, 1s. 6d. cloth.

Stevenson and Osbourne.—THE WRONG BOX. By ROBERT LOUIS STEVENSON and LLOYD OSBOURNE. Cr. 8vo., 3s. 6d.

Suttner.—LAY DOWN YOUR ARMS *Die Waffen Nieder:* The Autobiography of Martha Tilling. By BERTHA VON SUTTNER. Translated by T. HOLMES. Cr. 8vo., 1s. 6d.

Trollope.—Works by ANTHONY TROLLOPE.
THE WARDEN. Cr. 8vo., 1s. 6d.
BARCHESTER TOWERS. Cr. 8vo., 1s. 6d.

TRUE, A, RELATION OF THE TRAVELS AND PERILOUS ADVENTURES OF MATHEW DUDGEON, Gentleman: Wherein is truly set down the Manner of his Taking, the Long Time of his Slavery in Algiers, and Means of his Delivery. Written by Himself, and now for the first time printed Cr. 8vo., 5s.

Walford.—Works by L. B. WALFORD.
MR. SMITH : a Part of his Life. Crown 8vo., 2s. 6d.
THE BABY'S GRANDMOTHER. Crown 8vo., 2s. 6d
COUSINS. Crown 8vo. 2s. 6d.
TROUBLESOME DAUGHTERS. Crown 8vo., 2s. 6d.
PAULINE. Crown 8vo. 2s. 6d.
DICK NETHERBY. Crown 8vo., 2s. 6d.
THE HISTORY OF A WEEK. Crown 8vo. 2s. 6d.
A STIFF-NECKED GENERATION. Crown 8vo. 2s. 6d.
NAN, and other Stories. Cr. 8vo., 2s. 6d.
THE MISCHIEF OF MONICA. Crown 8vo., 2s. 6d.
THE ONE GOOD GUEST. Cr. 8vo. 2s. 6d.
'PLOUGHED,' and other Stories. Crown 8vo., 6s.
THE MATCHMAKER. 3 Vols. Cr. 8vo.

West.—Works by B. B. WEST.
HALF-HOURS WITH THE MILLIONAIRES: Showing how much harder it is to spend a million than to make it. Cr. 8vo., 6s.
SIR SIMON VANDERPETTER, AND MINDING HIS ANCESTORS. Two Reformations. Crown 8vo., 5s.

Weyman.—Works by S. J. WEYMAN.
THE HOUSE OF THE WOLF. Cr. 8vo., 3s. 6d.
A GENTLEMAN OF FRANCE. Cr. 8vo., 6s.

Popular Science (Natural History, &c.).

Butler.—OUR HOUSEHOLD INSECTS. An Account of the Insect-Pests found in Dwelling-Houses. By EDWARD A. BUTLER, B.A., B.Sc. (Lond.). With 113 Illustrations. Crown 8vo., 6s.

Furneaux.—Works by W. FURNEAUX.

THE OUTDOOR WORLD; or, The Young Collector's Handbook. With 18 Plates, 16 of which are coloured, and 549 Illustrations in the Text. Crown 8vo., 7s. 6d.

BUTTERFLIES AND MOTHS (British). With 12 coloured Plates and 241 Illustrations in the Text. Crown 8vo., 10s. 6d. net.

Hartwig.—Works by Dr. GEORGE HARTWIG.
THE SEA AND ITS LIVING WONDERS. With 12 Plates and 303 Woodcuts. 8vo., 7s. net.
THE TROPICAL WORLD. With 8 Plates and 172 Woodcuts. 8vo., 7s. net.
THE POLAR WORLD. With 3 Maps, 8 Plates and 85 Woodcuts. 8vo., 7s. net.
THE SUBTERRANEAN WORLD. With 3 Maps and 80 Woodcuts. 8vo., 7s. net.
THE AERIAL WORLD. With Map, 8 Plates and 60 Woodcuts. 8vo., 7s. net.

Popular Science (Natural History, &c.).

Hartwig.—Works by Dr. GEORGE HARTWIG—*continued.*

HEROES OF THE POLAR WORLD. 19 Illustrations. Crown 8vo., 2s.

WONDERS OF THE TROPICAL FORESTS. 40 Illustrations. Crown 8vo., 2s.

WORKERS UNDER THE GROUND. 29 Illustrations. Crown 8vo., 2s.

MARVELS OVER OUR HEADS. 29 Illustrations. Crown 8vo., 2s.

SEA MONSTERS AND SEA BIRDS. 75 Illustrations. Crown 8vo., 2s. 6d.

DENIZENS OF THE DEEP. 117 Illustrations. Crown 8vo., 2s. 6d.

VOLCANOES AND EARTHQUAKES. 30 Illustrations. Crown 8vo., 2s. 6d.

WILD ANIMALS OF THE TROPICS. 66 Illustrations. Crown 8vo., 3s. 6d.

Helmholtz.—POPULAR LECTURES ON SCIENTIFIC SUBJECTS. By HERMANN VON HELMHOLTZ. With 68 Woodcuts. 2 vols. Crown 8vo., 3s. 6d. each.

Proctor.—Works by RICHARD A. PROCTOR.

LIGHT SCIENCE FOR LEISURE HOURS. Familiar Essays on Scientific Subjects. 3 vols. Crown 8vo., 5s. each.

CHANCE AND LUCK: a Discussion of the Laws of Luck, Coincidence, Wagers, Lotteries and the Fallacies of Gambling, &c. Cr. 8vo., 2s. boards, 2s. 6d. cloth.

ROUGH WAYS MADE SMOOTH. Familiar Essays on Scientific Subjects. Silver Library Edition. Crown 8vo., 3s. 6d.

PLEASANT WAYS IN SCIENCE. Cr. 8vo., 5s. Silver Library Edition. Crown 8vo., 3s. 6d.

THE GREAT PYRAMID, OBSERVATORY, TOMB AND TEMPLE. With Illustrations. Crown 8vo., 5s.

NATURE STUDIES. By R. A. PROCTOR, GRANT ALLEN, A. WILSON, T. FOSTER and E. CLODD. Crown 8vo., 5s. Silver Library Edition. Crown 8vo., 3s. 6d.

LEISURE READINGS. By R. A. PROCTOR, E. CLODD, A. WILSON, T. FOSTER, and A. C. RANYARD. Cr. 8vo., 5s.

Stanley.—A FAMILIAR HISTORY OF BIRDS. By E. STANLEY, D.D., formerly Bishop of Norwich. With Illustrations. Cr. 8vo., 3s. 6d.

Wood.—Works by the Rev. J. G. WOOD.

HOMES WITHOUT HANDS : a Description of the Habitation of Animals, classed according to the Principle of Construction. With 140 Illustrations. 8vo., 7s. net.

INSECTS AT HOME : a Popular Account of British Insects, their Structure, Habits and Transformations. With 700 Illustrations. 8vo., 7s. net.

INSECTS ABROAD : a Popular Account of Foreign Insects, their Structure, Habits and Transformations. With 600 Illustrations. 8vo., 7s. net.

BIBLE ANIMALS : a Description of every Living Creature mentioned in the Scriptures. With 112 Illustrations. 8vo., 7s. net.

PETLAND REVISITED. With 33 Illustrations. Cr. 8vo., 3s. 6d.

OUT OF DOORS ; a Selection of Original Articles on Practical Natural History. With 11 Illustrations. Cr. 8vo., 3s. 6d.

STRANGE DWELLINGS : a Description of the Habitations of Animals, abridged from 'Homes without Hands'. With 60 Illustrations. Cr. 8vo., 3s. 6d.

BIRD LIFE OF THE BIBLE. 32 Illustrations. Cr. 8vo., 3s. 6d.

WONDERFUL NESTS. 30 Illustrations. Cr. 8vo., 3s. 6d.

HOMES UNDER THE GROUND. 28 Illustrations. Cr. 8vo., 3s. 6d.

WILD ANIMALS OF THE BIBLE. 29 Illustrations. Cr. 8vo., 3s. 6d.

DOMESTIC ANIMALS OF THE BIBLE. 23 Illustrations. Cr. 8vo., 3s. 6d.

THE BRANCH BUILDERS. 28 Illustrations. Cr. 8vo., 2s. 6d.

SOCIAL HABITATIONS AND PARASITIC NESTS. 18 Illustrations. Cr. 8vo., 2s.

Works of Reference.

Maunder's (Samuel) Treasuries.

BIOGRAPHICAL TREASURY. With Supplement brought down to 1889. By Rev. JAMES WOOD. Fcp. 8vo., 6s.

TREASURY OF NATURAL HISTORY : or, Popular Dictionary of Zoology. With 900 Woodcuts. Fcp. 8vo., 6s.

TREASURY OF GEOGRAPHY, Physical, Historical, Descriptive, and Political. With 7 Maps and 16 Plates. Fcp. 8vo., 6s.

THE TREASURY OF BIBLE KNOWLEDGE. By the Rev. J. AYRE, M.A. With 5 Maps, 15 Plates, and 300 Woodcuts. Fcp. 8vo., 6s.

HISTORICAL TREASURY : Outlines of Universal History, Separate Histories of all Nations. Fcp. 8vo., 6s.

TREASURY OF KNOWLEDGE AND LIBRARY OF REFERENCE. Comprising an English Dictionary and Grammar, Universal Gazeteer, Classical Dictionary, Chronology, Law Dictionary, &c. Fcp. 8vo., 6s.

Maunder's (Samuel) Treasuries —*continued.*

SCIENTIFIC AND LITERARY TREASURY. Fcp. 8vo., 6s.

THE TREASURY OF BOTANY. Edited by J. LINDLEY, F.R.S., and T. MOORE, F.L.S. With 274 Woodcuts and 20 Steel Plates. 2 vols. Fcp. 8vo., 12s.

Roget.--THESAURUS OF ENGLISH WORDS AND PHRASES. Classified and Arranged so as to Facilitate the Expression of Ideas and assist in Literary Composition. By PETER MARK ROGET, M.D., F.R.S. Recomposed throughout, enlarged and improved, partly from the Author's Notes, and with a full Index, by the Author's Son, JÒHN LEWIS ROGET. Crown 8vo., 10s. 6d.

Willich.—POPULAR TABLES for giving information for ascertaining the value of Lifehold, Leasehold, and Church Property, the Public Funds, &c. By CHARLES M. WILLICH. Edited by H. BENCE JONES. Crown 8vo., 10s. 6d.

Children's Books.

Crake.—Works by Rev. A. D. CRAKE.

EDWY THE FAIR ; or, the First Chronicle of Æscendune. Crown 8vo., 2s. 6d.

ALFGAR THE DANE: or, the Second Chronicle of Æscendune. Cr. 8vo., 2s. 6d.

THE RIVAL HEIRS : being the Third and Last Chronicle of Æscendune. Cr. 8vo., 2s. 6d.

THE HOUSE OF WALDERNE. A Tale of the Cloister and the Forest in the Days of the Barons' Wars. Crown 8vo., 2s. 6d.

BRIAN FITZ-COUNT. A Story of Wallingford Castle and Dorchester Abbey. Cr. 8vo., 2s. 6d.

Ingelow.—VERY YOUNG, AND QUITE ANOTHER STORY. Two Stories. By JEAN INGELOW. Crown 8vo., 2s. 6d.

Lang.—Works edited by ANDREW LANG.

THE BLUE FAIRY BOOK. With 138 Illustrations by H. J. FORD and G. P. JACOMB HOOD. Crown 8vo., 6s.

Lang.—Works edited by ANDREW LANG —*continued.*

THE RED FAIRY BOOK. With 100 Illustrations by H, J. FORD and LANCELOT SPEED. Cr. 8vo., 6s.

THE GREEN FAIRY BOOK. With 101 Illustrations by H. J. FORD and L. BOGLE. Crown 8vo., 6s.

THE YELLOW FAIRY BOOK. With 104 Illustrations by H. J. FORD. Crown 8vo., 6s.

THE BLUE POETRY BOOK. With 100 Illustrations by H. J. FORD and LANCELOT SPEED. Crown 8vo., 6s.

THE BLUE POETRY BOOK. School Edition, without Illustrations. Fcp. 8vo., 2s. 6d.

THE TRUE STORY BOOK. With 66 Illustrations by H. J. FORD, LUCIEN DAVIS, C. H. M. KERR, LANCELOT SPEED, and LOCKHART BOGLE. Crown 8vo., 6s.

Children's Books—*continued*.

Meade.—Works by L. T. MEADE.
DADDY'S BOY. Illustrated. Crown 8vo., 3*s.* 6*d.*
DEB AND THE DUCHESS. Illustrated. Crown 8vo., 3*s.* 6*d.*

Stevenson.—A CHILD'S GARDEN OF VERSES. By ROBERT LOUIS STEVENSON. Small fcp. 8vo., 5*s.*

Molesworth.—Works by Mrs. MOLESWORTH.
SILVERTHORNS. Illustrated. Cr. 8vo., 5*s.*
THE PALACE IN THE GARDEN. Illustrated. Crown 8vo., 5*s.*
NEIGHBOURS. Illus. Crown 8vo., 2*s.* 6*d.*

Longmans' Series of Books for Girls.

Crown 8vo., price 2*s.* 6*d.* each

ATELIER (THE) DU LYS : or an Art Student in the Reign of Terror.

BY THE SAME AUTHOR.

MADEMOISELLE MORI : a Tale of Modern Rome.

THAT CHILD. Illustrated by GORDON BROWNE.

UNDER A CLOUD.

THE FIDDLER OF LUGAU. With Illustrations by W. RALSTON.

A CHILD OF THE REVOLUTION. With Illustrations by C. J. STANILAND.

HESTER'S VENTURE.

IN THE OLDEN TIME : a Tale of the Peasant War in Germany.

THE YOUNGER SISTER.

ATHERSTONE PRIORY. By L. N. COMYN.

THE THIRD MISS ST. QUENTIN. By Mrs. MOLESWORTH.

THE STORY OF A SPRING MORNING, &c. By Mrs. MOLESWORTH. Illustrated.

NEIGHBOURS. By Mrs. MOLESWORTH. Illustrated.

VERY YOUNG ; and QUITE ANOTHER STORY. Two Stories. By JEAN INGELOW.

KEITH DERAMORE. By the Author of ' Miss Molly '.

SIDNEY. By MARGARET DELAND.

LAST WORDS TO GIRLS ON LIFE AT SCHOOL AND AFTER SCHOOL. By Mrs. W. GREY.

The Silver Library.

CROWN 8vo. 3*s.* 6*d.* EACH VOLUME.

Arnold's (Sir Edwin) Seas and Lands. With 71 Illustrations. 3*s.* 6*d.*

Baker's (Sir S. W.) Eight Years in Ceylon. With 6 Illustrations. 3*s.* 6*d.*

Baker's (Sir S. W.) Rifle and Hound in Ceylon. With 6 Illustrations. 3*s.* 6*d.*

Baring-Gould's (Rev. S.) Curious Myths of the Middle Ages. 3*s.* 6*d.*

Baring-Gould's (Rev. S.) Origin and Development of Religious Belief. 2 vols. 3*s.* 6*d.* each.

Brassey's (Lady) A Voyage in the ' Sunbeam '. With 66 Illustrations. 3*s.* 6*d.*

Clodd's (E.) Story of Creation : a Plain Account of Evolution. With 77 Illustrations. 3*s.* 6*d.*

Conybeare (Rev. W. J.) and Howson's (Very Rev. J. S.) Life and Epistles of St. Paul. 46 Illustrations. 3*s.* 6*d.*

Dougall's (L.) Beggars All ; a Novel. 3*s.* 6*d.*

Doyle's (A. Conan) Micah Clarke : a Tale of Monmouth's Rebellion. 3*s.* 6*d.*

Doyle's (A. Conan) The Captain of the Polestar, and other Tales. 3*s.* 6*d.*

Froude's (J. A.) Short Studies on Great Subjects. 4 vols. 3*s.* 6*d.* each.

Froude's (J. A.) Cæsar : a Sketch. 3*s.* 6*d.*

Froude's (J. A.) Thomas Carlyle : a History of his Life.
1795-1835. 2 vols. 7*s.*
1834-1881. 2 vols. 7*s.*

Froude's (J. A.) The Two Chiefs of Dunboy : an Irish Romance of the Last Century. 3*s.* 6*d.*

Froude's (J. A.) The History of England, from the Fall of Wolsey to the Defeat of the Spanish Armada. 12 vols. 3*s.* 6*d.* each.

Gleig's (Rev. G. R.) Life of the Duke of Wellington. With Portrait. 3*s.* 6*d.*

The Silver Library—*continued.*

Haggard's (H. R.) She: A History of Adventure. 32 Illustrations. 3*s.* 6*d.*

Haggard's (H. R.) Allan Quatermain. With 20 Illustrations. 3*s.* 6*d.*

Haggard's (H. R.) Colonel Quaritch, V.C. : a Tale of Country Life. 3*s.* 6*d.*

Haggard's (H. R.) Cleopatra. With 29 Full-page Illustrations. 3*s.* 6*d.*

Haggard's (H. R.) Eric Brighteyes. With 51 Illustrations. 3*s.* 6*d.*

Haggard's (H. R.) Beatrice. 3*s.* 6*d.*

Haggard's (H. R.) Allan's Wife. With 34 Illustrations. 3*s.* 6*d.*

Haggard's (H. R.) The Witch's Head. With Illustrations. 3*s.* 6*d.*

Haggard's (H. R.) Mr. Meeson's Will. With Illustrations. 3*s.* 6*d.*

Haggard's (H. R.) Dawn. With 16 Illustrations. 3*s.* 6*d.*

Haggard's (H. R.) and Lang's (A.) The World's Desire. With 27 Illustrations. 3*s.* 6*d.*

Harte's (Bret) In the Carquinez Woods, and other Stories. 3*s.* 6*d.*

Helmholtz's (Hermann von) Popular Lectures on Scientific Subjects. With 68 Woodcuts. 2 vols. 3*s.* 6*d.* each.

Howitt's (W.) Visits to Remarkable Places. 80 Illustrations. 3*s.* 6*d.*

Jefferies' (R.) The Story of My Heart: My Autobiography. With Portrait. 3*s.* 6*d.*

Jefferies' (R.) Field and Hedgerow. Last Essays of. With Portrait. 3*s.* 6*d.*

Jefferies' (R.) Red Deer. With 17 Illustrations by J. CHARLTON and H. TUNALY. 3*s.* 6*d.*

Jefferies' (R.) Wood Magic: a Fable. With Frontispiece and Vignette by E. V. B. 3*s.* 6*d.*

Jefferies' (R.) The Toilers of the Field. With Portrait from the Bust in Salisbury Cathedral. 3*s.* 6*d.*

Knight's (E. F.) The Cruise of the 'Alerte': the Narrative of a Search for Treasure on the Desert Island of Trinidad. With 2 Maps and 23 Illustrations. 3*s.* 6*d.*

Lang's (A.) Custom and Myth: Studies of Early Usage and Belief. 3*s.* 6*d.*

Lees (J. A.) and Clutterbuck's (W. J.) B.C. 1887, A Ramble in British Columbia. With Maps and 75 Illustrations. 3*s.* 6*d.*

Macaulay's (Lord) Essays and Lays of Ancient Rome. With Portrait and Illustrations. 3*s.* 6*d.*

Macleod (H. D.) The Elements of Banking. 3*s.* 6*d.*

Marshman's (J. C.) Memoirs of Sir Henry Havelock. 3*s.* 6*d.*

Max Müller's (F.) India, what can it teach us? 3*s.* 6*d.*

Max Müller's (F.) Introduction to the Science of Religion. 3*s.* 6*d.*

Merivale's (Dean) History of the Romans under the Empire. 8 vols. 3*s.* 6*d.* ea.

Mill's (J. S.) Political Economy. 3*s.* 6*d.*

Mill's (J. S.) System of Logic. 3*s.* 6*d.*

Milner's (Geo.) Country Pleasures. 3*s.* 6*d.*

Phillipps-Wolley's (C.) Snap: a Legend of the Lone Mountain. With 13 Illustrations. 3*s.* 6*d.*

Proctor's (R. A.) The Orbs Around Us. Essays on the Moon and Planets, Metors and Comets, the Sun and Coloured Pairs of Suns. 3*s.* 6*d.*

Proctor's (R. A.) The Expanse of Heaven. Essays on the Wonders of the Firmament. 3*s.* 6*d.*

Proctor's (R. A.) Other Worlds than Ours. 3*s.* 6*d.*

Proctor's (R. A.) Rough Ways made Smooth. 3*s.* 6*d.*

Proctor's (R. A.) Pleasant Ways in Science. 3*s.* 6*d.*

Proctor's (R. A.) Myths and Marvels of Astronomy. 3*s.* 6*d.*

Proctor's (R. A.) Nature Studies. 3*s.* 6*d.*

Rossetti's (Maria F.) A Shadow of Dante: being an Essay towards studying Himself, his World and his Pilgrimage. With Frontispiece by DANTE GABRIEL ROSSETTI. 3*s.* 6*d.*

Smith's (R. Bosworth) Carthage and the Carthaginians. 3*s.* 6*d.*

Stanley's (Bishop) Familiar History of Birds. 160 Illustrations. 3*s.* 6*d.*

Stevenson (Robert Louis) and Osbourne's (Lloyd) The Wrong Box. 3*s.* 6*d.*

Weyman's (Stanley J.) The House of the Wolf: a Romance. 3*s.* 6*d.*

Wood's (Rev. J. G.) Petland Revisited. With 33 Illustrations. 3*s.* 6*d.*

Wood's (Rev. J. G.) Strange Dwellings. With 60 Illustrations. 3*s.* 6*d.*

Wood's (Rev. J. G.) Out of Doors. 11 Illustrations. 3*s.* 6*d.*

Cookery, Domestic Management, &c.

Acton.—MODERN COOKERY. By ELIZA ACTON. With 150 Woodcuts. Fcp. 8vo., 4s. 6d.

Bull.—Works by THOMAS BULL, M.D.
HINTS TO MOTHERS ON THE MANAGE-MENT OF THEIR HEALTH DURING THE PERIOD OF PREGNANCY. Fcp. 8vo., 1s. 6d.
THE MATERNAL MANAGEMENT OF CHILDREN IN HEALTH AND DISEASE. Fcp. 8vo., 1s. 6d.

De Salis.—Works by Mrs. DE SALIS.
CAKES AND CONFECTIONS À LA MODE. Fcp. 8vo., 1s. 6d.
DOGS : a Manual for Amateurs. Fcp. 8vo.,
DRESSED GAME AND POULTRY À LA MODE. Fcp. 8vo., 1s. 6d.
DRESSED VEGETABLES À LA MODE. Fcp. 8vo., 1s. 6d.
DRINKS À LA MODE. Fcp. 8vo., 1s. 6d.
ENTRÉES À LA MODE. Fcp. 8vo., 1s. 6d.
FLORAL DECORATIONS. Suggestions and Descriptions. Fcp. 8vo., 1s. 6d.
NATIONAL VIANDS. Fcp. 8vo.
[In the Press.
NEW-LAID EGGS : Hints for Amateur Poultry Rearers. Fcp. 8vo., 1s. 6d.
OYSTERS À LA MODE. Fcp. 8vo., 1s. 6d.

De Salis.—Works by Mrs. DE SALIS—continued.
PUDDINGS AND PASTRY À LA MODE. Fcp. 8vo., 1s. 6d.
SAVOURIES À LA MODE. Fcp. 8vo., 1s. 6d.
SOUPS AND DRESSED FISH À LA MODE. Fcp. 8vo., 1s. 6d.
SWEETS AND SUPPER DISHES À LA MODE. Fcp. 8vo., 1s. 6d.
TEMPTING DISHES FOR SMALL IN-COMES. Fcp. 8vo., 1s. 6d.
WRINKLES AND NOTIONS FOR EVERY HOUSEHOLD. Cr. 8vo., 1s. 6d.

Lear.—MAIGRE COOKERY. By H. L. SIDNEY LEAR. 16mo., 2s.

Poole.—COOKERY FOR THE DIABETIC. By W. H. and Mrs. POOLE. With Preface by Dr. PAVY. Fcp. 8vo., 2s. 6d.

Walker.—A HANDBOOK FOR MOTHERS: being Simple Hints to Women on the Management of their Health during Pregnancy and Confinement, together with Plain Directions as to the Care of Infants. By JANE H. WALKER, L.R.C.P. and L.M., L.R.C.S. and M.D. (Brux.). Cr. 8vo., 2s. 6d.

West.—THE MOTHER'S MANUAL OF CHILDREN'S DISEASES. By CHARLES WEST, M.D. Fcp. 8vo., 2s. 6d.

Miscellaneous and Critical Works.

Allingham.—VARIETIES IN PROSE. By WILLIAM ALLINGHAM. 3 vols. Cr. 8vo, 18s. (Vols. 1 and 2, Rambles, by PATRICIUS WALKER. Vol. 3, Irish Sketches, etc.)

Armstrong.—ESSAYS AND SKETCHES. By EDMUND J. ARMSTRONG. Fcp. 8vo., 5s.

Bagehot.—LITERARY STUDIES. By WALTER BAGEHOT. 2 vols. 8vo., 28s.

Baring-Gould.—CURIOUS MYTHS OF THE MIDDLE AGES. By Rev. S. BARING-GOULD. Crown 8vo., 3s. 6d.

Battye.—PICTURES IN PROSE OF NATURE, WILD SPORT, AND HUMBLE LIFE. By AUBYN TREVOR BATTYE, B.A. Crown 8vo., 6s.

Baynes.—SHAKESPEARE STUDIES, AND OTHER ESSAYS. By the late THOMAS SPENCER BAYNES, LL.B., LL.D. With a biographical Preface by Prof. LEWIS CAMPBELL. Crown 8vo., 7s. 6d.

Boyd ('A. K. H. B.').—Works by A. K. H. BOYD, D.D., LL.D.
And see MISCELLANEOUS THEOLO-GICAL WORKS, p. 24.
AUTUMN HOLIDAYS OF A COUNTRY PARSON. Crown 8vo., 3s. 6d.
COMMONPLACE PHILOSOPHER. Crown 8vo., 3s. 6d.
CRITICAL ESSAYS OF A COUNTRY PARSON. Crown 8vo., 3s. 6d.
EAST COAST DAYS AND MEMORIES. Crown 8vo., 3s. 6d.
LANDSCAPES, CHURCHES AND MORA-LITIES. Crown 8vo., 3s. 6d.
LEISURE HOURS IN TOWN. Crown 8vo., 3s. 6d.
LESSONS OF MIDDLE AGE. Cr.8vo.,3s.6d.
OUR LITTLE LIFE. Two Series. Cr. 8vo., 3s. 6d. each.
OUR HOMELY COMEDY: AND TRAGEDY. Crown 8vo., 3s. 6d.
RECREATIONS OF A COUNTRY PARSON. Three Series. Cr. 8vo., 3s. 6d. each. Also First Series. Popular Ed. 8vo., 6d.

Miscellaneous and Critical Works—*continued.*

Butler.—Works by SAMUEL BUTLER.
EREWHON. Cr. 8vo., 5*s*.
THE FAIR HAVEN. A Work in Defence of the Miraculous Element in our Lord's Ministry. Cr. 8vo., 7*s*. 6*d*.
LIFE AND HABIT. An Essay after a Completer View of Evolution. Cr. 8vo., 7*s*. 6*d*
EVOLUTION, OLD AND NEW. Cr. 8vo., 10*s*. 6*d*.
ALPS AND SANCTUARIES OF PIEDMONT AND CANTON TICINO. Illustrated. Pott 4to., 10*s*.6*d*.
LUCK, OR CUNNING, AS THE MAIN MEANS OF ORGANIC MODIFICATION? Cr. 8vo., 7*s*. 6*d*.
EX VOTO. An Account of the Sacro Monte or New Jerusalem at Varallo-Sesia. Crown 8vo., 10*s*. 6*d*.

Francis.—JUNIUS REVEALED By his surviving Grandson, H. R. FRANCIS, M.A., late Fellow of St. John's College, Cambridge. 8vo., 6*s*.

Hodgson. — OUTCAST ESSAYS AND VERSE TRANSLATIONS. By H. SHADWORTH HODGSON. Crown 8vo., 8*s*. 6*d*.

Hullah.—Works by J. HULLAH, LL.D.
COURSE OF LECTURES ON THE HISTORY OF MODERN MUSIC. 8vo., 8*s*.6*d*.
COURSE OF LECTURES ON THE TRANSITION PERIOD OF MUSICAL HISTORY. 8vo., 10*s*. 6*d*.

Jefferies.—Works by R. JEFFERIES.
FIELD AND HEDGEROW : last Essays. With Portrait. Crown 8vo., 3*s*. 6*d*.
THE STORY OF MY HEART : With Portrait and New Preface by C. J. LONGMAN. Crown 8vo., 3*s*. 6*d*.
RED DEER. With 17 Illustrations. Cr. 8vo., 3*s*. 6*d*.
THE TOILERS OF THE FIELD. With Portrait. Crown 8vo., 3*s*. 6*d*.
WOOD MAGIC. With Frontispiece and Vignette by E. V. B. Cr. 8vo., 3*s*. 6*d*.

Johnson.—THE PATENTEE'S MANUAL : a Treatise on the Law and Practice of Letters Patent. By J. & J. H. JOHNSON, Patent Agents, &c. 8vo., 10*s*. 6*d*.

Lang.—Works by ANDREW LANG.
LETTERS TO DEAD AUTHORS. Fcp. 8vo., 2*s*. 6*d*. net.
LETTERS ON LITERATURE. Fcp. 8vo., 2*s*. 6*d*. net.
BOOKS AND BOOKMEN. With 19 Illustrations. Fcp. 8vo., 2*s*. 6*d*. net.
OLD FRIENDS. Fcp. 8vo., 2*s*. 6*d*. net.
COCK LANE AND COMMON SENSE. Fcp. 8vo., 6*s*. 6*d*. net.

Leonard.—THE CAMEL : Its Uses and Management. By Major ARTHUR GLYN LEONARD. Royal 8vo., 21*s*. net.

Macfarren.—LECTURES ON HARMONY. By Sir GEO. A. MACFARREN. 8vo., 12*s*.

Max Müller.—Works by F. MAX MÜLLER.
INDIA : WHAT CAN IT TEACH US ? Cr. 8vo., 3*s*. 6*d*.
CHIPS FROM A GERMAN WORKSHOP. New Edition in 4 Vols. Vol. I., Recent Essays and Addresses. Crown 8vo., 6*s*. 6*d*. net. (*Ready*).
In Preparation—Vol. II., Biographical Essays; Vol. III., Essays on Language and Literature ; Vol. IV., Essays on the Sciences of Language, of Thought, and of Mythology.

Mendelssohn.—THE LETTERS OF FELIX MENDELSSOHN. Translated by Lady WALLACE. 2 vols. Cr. 8vo., 10*s*.

Milner.—Works by GEORGE MILNER.
COUNTRY PLEASURES : the Chronicle of a Year chiefly in a Garden. Cr. 8vo., 3*s*. 6*d*.
STUDIES OF NATURE ON THE COAST OF ARRAN. With Illustrations by W. NOEL JOHNSON. 16mo., 6*s*. 6*d*. net.

Perring.—HARD KNOTS IN SHAKESPEARE. By Sir PHILIP PERRING, Bart. 8vo. 7*s*. 6*d*.

Proctor.—Works by R. A. PROCTOR.
STRENGTH AND HAPPINESS. With 9 Illustrations. Crown 8vo., 5*s*.
STRENGTH : How to get Strong and keep Strong, with Chapters on Rowing and Swimming, Fat, Age, and the Waist. With 9 Illus. Cr. 8vo, 2*s*.

Richardson.—NATIONAL HEALTH. A Review of the Works of Sir Edwin Chadwick, K.C.B. By Sir B. W. RICHARDSON, M.D. Cr. 8vo., 4*s*. 6*d*.

Rossetti.—A SHADOW OF DANTE : being an Essay towards studying Himself, his World, and his Pilgrimage. By MARIA FRANCESCA ROSSETTI. Cr. 8vo., 3*s*. 6*d*.

Southey.—CORRESPONDENCE WITH CAROLINE BOWLES. By R. SOUTHEY. Edited by E. DOWDEN. 8vo., 14*s*.

Wallaschek.—PRIMITIVE MUSIC : an Inquiry into the Origin and Development of Music, Songs, Instruments, Dances, and Pantomimes of Savage Races. By RICHARD WALLASCHEK. With Musical Examples. 8vo., 12*s*. 6*d*.

West.—WILLS, AND HOW NOT TO MAKE THEM. With a Selection of Leading Cases. By B. B. WEST. Fcp. 8vo., 2*s*. 6*d*.

Miscellaneous Theological Works.

₊ For Church of England and Roman Catholic Works see MESSRS. LONGMANS & CO.'S
Special Catalogues.

Boyd.—Works by A. K. H. BOYD, D.D., First Minister of St. Andrews, author of 'Recreations of a Country Parson,' &c.

COUNCIL AND COMFORT FROM A CITY PULPIT. Crown 8vo., 3s. 6d.

SUNDAY AFTERNOONS IN THE PARISH CHURCH OF A SCOTTISH UNIVERSITY CITY. Crown 8vo., 3s. 6d.

CHANGED ASPECTS OF UNCHANGED TRUTHS. Crown 8vo., 3s. 6d.

GRAVER THOUGHTS OF A COUNTRY PARSON. Three Series. Crown 8vo., 3s. 6d. each.

PRESENT DAY THOUGHTS. Crown 8vo., 3s. 6d.

SEASIDE MUSINGS. Cr. 8vo., 3s. 6d.

'TO MEET THE DAY' through the Christian Year ; being a Text of Scripture, with an Original Meditation and a Short Selection in Verse for Every Day. Crown 8vo., 4s. 6d.

De La Saussaye.—A MANUAL OF THE SCIENCE OF RELIGION. By Prof. CHANTEPIE DE LA SAUSSAYE. Translated by Mrs. COLYER FERGUSSON (née MAX MULLER). Crown 8vo.. 12s. 6d.

Kalisch.—Works by M. M. KALISCH, BIBLE STUDIES. Part I. The Prophecies of Balaam. 8vo., 10s. 6d. Part II. The Book of Jonah. 8vo., 10s. 6d.

COMMENTARY ON THE OLD TESTAMENT: with a new Translation. Vol. I. Genesis. 8vo., 18s. Or adapted for the General Reader. 12s. Vol. II. Exodus. 15s. Or adapted for the General Reader. 12s. Vol. III. Leviticus, Part I. 15s. Or adapted for the General Reader. 8s. Vol. IV. Leviticus, Part II. 15s. Or adapted for the General Reader. 8s.

Martineau.—Works by JAMES MARTINEAU, D.D., LL.D.

HOURS OF THOUGHT ON SACRED THINGS. Two Volumes of Sermons. Crown 8vo., 7s. 6d.

ENDEAVOURS AFTER THE CHRISTIAN LIFE. Discourses. Cr. 8vo., 7s. 6d.

THE SEAT OF AUTHORITY IN RELIGION. 8vo., 14s.

ESSAYS, REVIEWS, AND ADDRESSES. 4 Vols. Crown 8vo., 7s. 6d. each.
I. Personal ; Political.
II. Ecclesiastical ; Historical.
III. Theological ; Philosophical.
IV. Academical ; Religious

HOME PRAYERS, with Two Services for Public Worship. Crown 8vo. 3s. 6d.

Macdonald.—Works by GEORGE MACDONALD, LL.D.

UNSPOKEN SERMONS. Three Series. Crown 8vo., 3s. 6d. each.

THE MIRACLES OF OUR LORD. Crown 8vo., 3s. 6d.

A BOOK OF STRIFE, IN THE FORM OF THE DIARY OF AN OLD SOUL : Poems 18mo., 6s.

Max Müller.—Works by F. MAX MULLER.

HIBBERT LECTURES ON THE ORIGIN AND GROWTH OF RELIGION, as illustrated by the Religions of India. Crown 8vo., 7s. 6d.

INTRODUCTION TO THE SCIENCE OF RELIGION : Four Lectures delivered at the Royal Institution. Cr. 8vo. , 3s. 6d.

NATURAL RELIGION. The Gifford Lectures, delivered before the University of Glasgow in 1888. Cr. 8vo., 10s. 6d.

PHYSICAL RELIGION. The Gifford Lectures, delivered before the University of Glasgow in 1890. Cr. 8vo., 10s. 6d.

ANTHROPOLOGICAL RELIGION. The Gifford Lectures, delivered before the University of Glasgow in 1891. Cr. 8vo., 10s. 6d.

THEOSOPHY OR PSYCHOLOGICAL RELIGION. The Gifford Lectures, delivered before the University of Glasgow in 1892. Cr. 8vo., 10s. 6d.

THREE LECTURES ON THE VEDANTA PHILOSOPHY, delivered at the Royal Institution in March, 1894. 8vo., 5s.

Scholler.—A CHAPTER OF CHURCH HISTORY FROM SOUTH GERMANY: being Passages from the Life of Johann Evangelist Georg Lutz, formerly Parish Priest and Dean in Oberroth, Bavaria. By L. W. SCHOLLER. Translated from the German by W. WALLIS. Crown 8vo., 3s. 6d.

SUPERNATURAL RELIGION : an Inquiry into the Reality of Divine Revelation. 3 vols. 8vo., 36s.

REPLY (A) TO DR. LIGHTFOOT'S ESSAYS. By the Author of 'Supernatural Religion'. 8vo., 6s.

THE GOSPEL ACCORDING TO ST: PETER: a Study. By the Author of 'Supernatural Religion'. 8vo., 6s.

50,000—11/94.   ABERDEEN UNIVERSITY PRESS.